Bri taini's

KV-418-427

PELICAN BOOKS

BRITAIN AND THE WORLD
ECONOMY

Born in Glasgow in 1925, Dr Livingstone graduated
from Glasgow University in History and later took
London degrees in Economics. He spent two years
in the Home Civil Service before deciding to make
teaching his career. His most recent position has been
Lecturer in Management Studies at the Scottish Col-
lege of Commerce; upon its integration into the new
University of Strathclyde, he became Senior Lecturer,
and he is now a Reader in Commerce. Here he is able to
help in developing degree courses in the field of overseas trade, his special interest. Dr Livingstone has also
published various articles on management and marketing problems.

J. M. LIVINGSTONE

BRITAIN AND THE WORLD ECONOMY

PENGUIN BOOKS

Penguin Books Ltd, Harmondsworth, Middlesex, England
Penguin Books Inc., 7110 Ambassador Road, Baltimore, Maryland 21207, U.S.A.
Penguin Books Australia Ltd, Ringwood, Victoria, Australia

—

First published 1966
Reprinted 1969
Reprinted with minor revisions 1971

—

Copyright © J. M. Livingstone, 1966

—

Made and printed in Great Britain
by Richard Clay (The Chaucer Press) Ltd,
Bungay, Suffolk
Set in Monotype Times

CONTENTS

INTRODUCTION

The United Kingdom in a Changing World

THE two decades which have passed since the end of the Second World War have been a period of dramatic and at times uncomfortable change for the United Kingdom. While the importance of Britain in the world economy has declined substantially, the standard of living of the great majority of its inhabitants has improved dramatically. Neither process has ended. Indeed, neither process is absolutely inevitable, and the speed with which either goes on depends, at least in part, on the conscious decisions of the British Government and people.

The theme of this book is the extent to which Britain is adjusting to her new place in the world and the crises which accompany this adjustment. While the causes of a particular crisis, and the means either adopted or suggested to deal with it may at times be rather obscure to the man in the street, the basic factors which create both crisis and response are simple enough – often brutally simple. It is surely in the interest of everyone subjected to the vicissitudes of boom and credit squeeze, and all the other political and economic phenomena of Britain in the 1960s, to take rather more than a passing interest in the outside factors which cause and shape so much of the events in Britain.

It is the intention of this book at least to delineate some of these factors.

The United Kingdom – her past and present roles

The United Kingdom consists of a number of islands on the periphery of Europe. With a population of about fifty-three million in a world population exceeding three thousand million, her importance in the whole world economy might appear to be small.

Yet in spite of her small population, and her almost total lack of the raw materials vital for twentieth-century technology, the significance of the United Kingdom in the world economy is by no means negligible. With less than two per cent of the world's population she absorbs about fifteen per cent of all raw materials appearing in international trade and is responsible for about ten per cent of the exports of manufactures. For Britain's economic importance cannot be judged in isolation, but in the context of her relationships with other nations and regions of the world. These relationships are many and diverse. She is the centre of a political system, the Commonwealth, which has seen stronger days, but is still of some consequence in the political and economic groupings of the world. By virtue of this Commonwealth connexion she is a partner in Imperial Preference, a system of trade discrimination intended to channel trade, by preferential tariffs, among members of the Commonwealth numbering about one quarter of the world's population. The pound sterling, the internal currency of the United Kingdom, shares with gold and the American dollar the role of world international currencies. Britain is thus a world banker, with London as a world financial centre, rivalling New York, but without equal elsewhere in the world.

These are but a few of the worldwide responsibilities of the United Kingdom economy. In her more local status as a European power, Britain is a founder member of one of the two major trading blocs of Western Europe, the European Free Trade Association, and has sought membership of the other, the European Common Market. Whatever the geography of the situation may be, in technological and economic terms Britain is far from being an island economy: and every day which passes makes isolation from Europe less possible.

Membership of, or involvement in, the vast industrial, financial or economic groupings of the world economy produces strains and contradictions in the United Kingdom. With political and economic responsibilities of this nature, and since these responsibilities exceed her resources, Britain is scarcely a world power any longer, but she is not yet entirely a European power. As head of a Commonwealth whose future is uncertain, and as a world banker whose responsibilities in overseeing a worldwide currency system bring rewards in influence and prestige, she has the problems of a potentially overloaded economy. While the southern part of Britain is more and more a sector of the vast European industrial complex, the northern half and the smaller islands suffer the consequences of the magnetic attraction of this industrial grouping to the south, in terms of an ever threatening drain of manpower and industry.

In spite of her relatively small size, population and her inadequate national resources, Britain's involvement in so much of the world's economic activity gives her a role in the world that is out of all proportion to her size. But that role is tending to shrink, not because British power and wealth are declining in absolute terms, but rather because other factors are growing in importance. By the end of the century, for example, the British population will probably be only about one per cent of the rapidly expanding world population, and that fact alone would be enough to bring about a most profound change in the relative importance of Britain.

If it is unrealistic to discuss the world economy in detail without taking note of the various roles of the United Kingdom, it would be sheer foolishness to discuss the British economy in isolation from the world economy. More than for most nations, the prosperity of Britain depends on the state of the world economy. Britain's interest in promoting easier conditions of international trade, and indeed in every step which will make the world economy function more smoothly, is paramount. In the last resort the world economy could survive relatively unscathed if an economic catastrophe overtook the United Kingdom. Britain could scarcely survive in a hostile world economy.

Britain's commitments

Britain, then, is a nation with several roles in the world. Some of these have been imposed by history, some accepted voluntarily. To take but one example, though the present-day Commonwealth can be regarded as but a pale shade of the once powerful British Empire, the fact that that Empire once existed still has profound effects on British investment overseas and on British trade with many parts of the world. This legacy may at times give the British exporter an advantage over a trade rival thanks to old established links; conversely it may at times place him at a disadvantage if the imperial connexion ended in bitterness.

These conditions imposed by history are of fading significance, but they are not readily changeable by the individual merchant or the British Government. But there is another legacy, voluntarily accepted by Britain, of continuing responsibilities – some would say pretensions – towards former subject states of the Empire. This may for example impose additional burdens of taxation at home and commitments overseas, with the consequent danger of overstrain to the economy. Not the least of Britain's problems in competing in trade with, say, Germany or Japan may be the extent and expense of her involvement in problems throughout the world, and the possible detriment of this involvement to British commercial interests.

Thus far we have considered Britain's external commitments only; and, without entering into a discussion about whether the overseas policies of successive British governments since the Second World War have been worth their cost to her economy, we can at least acknowledge that any particular foreign policy will clearly affect the problems of the United Kingdom in her relations with the countries of the Commonwealth, Europe, or indeed any part of the world.

Quite apart from external commitments and aims, the British Government, whatever its political complexion, has certain very obvious goals inside Britain. Of these perhaps the most consequential is the maintenance of the welfare state and all its ramifications of full employment, adequate social security and so on. Just as British foreign policy involves heavy political and military expenditure, so too the objectives of the welfare state demand a high level of government expenditure and taxation. The consequent heavy pressure on the resources of the home economy is such that excessive demand and over-employment are likely to be rather more of a problem than lack of demand and hence unemployment.

An ambitious overseas policy and an ambitious internal policy are economically speaking excellent, if they result in the economy operating at a level which will create full employment. But if they overstrain the resources available, and go beyond full employment into inflation, then they make it difficult to secure a high rate of growth in the economy, and by rising prices affect Britain's ability to pay its way in the world. Despite persisting pockets, indeed regions, of under-employment, this has been the fate of Britain for a good deal of the past twenty years.

These problems are not unique to the United Kingdom. But they are rather more acute for Britain than for most nations.

The theme of this book is, as we have said, Britain's adjustment to her new role or roles in the world economy. It is written in the belief that, at the very least, an appreciation of some of the implications of the past and present roles of the United Kingdom is essential to an understanding of the problems facing Britain today.

Any of these roles will have ramifications on every other, and it would of course be unrealistic to imagine that one could examine any one role in isolation, and then pop it back, so to speak, into its own pigeon-hole. Nevertheless, to impose any sort of logical pattern it is necessary to do just that, and the pattern of the following chapters therefore deals with the separate roles somewhat in this manner.

The first chapter outlines some of the principles on which the world economy operates. Well over a hundred nations, of varying degrees of independence, power and responsibility, are free to conduct their economic policies to their own inclinations. The United Kingdom is one of these economies, still indeed one of the most powerful and influential, but one too which is more vulnerable than most to vagaries in the world economy. The two facts contained in that sentence have always to be reconciled by any British government. If the world economy really becomes what it has been at times in the past, an economic 'free for all', Britain could probably hold her own: but in view of her economic and political vulnerability, she would be the last to precipitate such a state of affairs.

Having examined at least in outline some of the salient points of the world economic system, we shall look at Britain's immediate responsibilities in the international monetary field, namely that of sustaining sterling as an international currency, used extensively in world trade and held as the chief form of international currency reserve by member nations of the Sterling Area. The mechanics of maintaining an international role for sterling involve the United Kingdom in a complicated pattern of international borrowing and lending. The complications and the limitations on the freedom of action of the British economy that this produces are not the least cause of the numerous sterling crises since the end of the Second World War.

After this study of the consequences of sterling's international role, it will be profitable to look a little more closely at Britain's balance of payments, which is at least in part shaped by sterling's unique position, and to note where our interests and markets lie.

A point which emerges from this discussion is the extent to which traditional concepts have been challenged by the dramatic developments in Europe in the last twenty years. The international role of sterling, and the massive investment in the Sterling Area and Commonwealth which appears to have been the pattern of the past, have now to be reconciled with the resurgence of Europe, which today challenges the importance of the super-powers of America and Russia, and is rapidly overhauling the Commonwealth and Sterling Area as a market for British exports. It is one of the tragedies of the postwar years that Britain, partly by circumstance but more by choice, has been excluded from a more active participation in continental Europe's recovery. Whether or not the efforts to secure a better foothold in the European economy succeed, there is no doubt that British prosperity for the rest of the century is intimately linked with the European Common Market; her relationship with Europe since the war must therefore be a central theme in any discussion of Britain's place in the world.

Passing on to the yet wider fields of international economics, we must examine the whole theme of international equilibrium – the attempts made during and after the Second World War to ensure that never again would nations find it necessary for their economic welfare to act in complete disregard of the interests of others. The avoidance of 'beggar my neighbour' policies, and the growing practice of international cooperation between the nations of the Western World have, in spite of vicissitudes, produced a chapter of success, although, as we shall see, a number of problems are looming up on the vexed issue of keeping world monetary reserves expanding at an appropriate rate.

Britain's interest in freer trade is a point which has been made often. The way in which the postwar world has tackled the problems of freeing trade is our next theme. Here again we see that the picture since the end of the war has been on the whole encouraging. Less encouraging, however, is the fact that Britain's interest in freer trade is not always matched by her ability to influence events towards this.

Finally we examine a problem that is potentially far more serious than the Cold War at its coldest – the problem of the world's rich and the world's poor. The gap between rich nations and poor is widening, with sinister implications of racial strife. Britain's capacity to solve this vast moral and political problem by herself is limited by her relatively small size and her apparent inability to overcome many of her own economic problems. But as leader of a multi-racial Commonwealth her influence in solving some of the problems of reconciling the privileged and the hungry may be out of all proportion to her size. In this task of reconciliation may lie Britain's greatest role for the remainder of the century.

This outline is a sketch map of where this book is intended to go, and the theme of its argument.

Chapter 1

THE INTERNATIONAL ECONOMY

SINCE this book is about Britain's part in the international economy, the first chapter is about some of the problems of the international economy and is illustrated by examples involving nations other than Britain. For we must understand what these problems are before we can sensibly discuss the British role in solving them. The chapter cannot be anything like comprehensive in its discussion of all the issues, but it can at least touch upon those of most consequence to Britain.

Then follows the question of choice in the world economy – the choice between 'good neighbour' policies of international co-operation and mutual consideration, on the one hand, and the international 'free for all' which is the alternative, and which could involve the United Kingdom in a fierce struggle for existence. For Britain's whole future depends on the extent of international good neighbourliness; and to convince the reader of this point is the whole purpose of this chapter.

Competing objectives

International economic problems, like most other economic problems, are matters of conflicting aims and alternative choices.

These problems can scarcely be of mere academic interest for anyone who lives within the United Kingdom, for our whole domestic and political situation is shaped by the circumstances of international economics, and our response to the problems of the world economy helps in turn to shape those problems. This somewhat trite statement is of course true of any nation, but for the United Kingdom, whose annual exports and imports each account for about one fifth of the entire national income, the relevance of this two-way relationship between domestic and international economic policy is immediate.

Any economic or political decision taken within Britain will therefore have international repercussions. Sometimes of course these will be so small as to be negligible, but sometimes they will be of considerable and unforeseen consequence. We can neither entirely ignore the external results of our domestic policies, nor can we allow ourselves to be absolutely inhibited from action by the thought of external effects. The same argument of course applies to the domestic actions of a nation like the United States whose activities will at times affect British interests.

What any nation may have to reckon on is the desirability of reconciling conflicting interests. Sometimes these conflicting interests most affect the nation originating the process in that the effects of its domestic actions are detrimental to its own external interests more than to any other nation. One example of this state of affairs is the situation with which we have all become familiar in recent years in the relationship between full employment on the one hand and a satisfactory balance of external trade and payments on the other.

A high level of investment in roads, factories and all types of capital equipment is a first prerequisite for steady growth in national wealth; a high level of public expenditure is necessary to meet the social, political and strategic objectives of most governments; and a surplus in the balance of trade may be a necessity if Britain wishes to maintain sterling's reputation as an internationally used currency. All of these objectives, as can be imagined, tend to produce not merely a high level of employment but, all too easily, inflation.

Once inflation begins to appear in an economy like Britain's, a satisfactory balance of payments becomes very difficult to achieve, for a fall in the internal value of sterling will be quickly matched by a fall in its external value.

In practice, inflation has never been an extreme problem in Britain since the end of the war, for the external sterling crisis has appeared, and has had to be dealt with, long before the internal

‚inflationary situation has got out of hand. In Chapter 2 some of these crises are examined in detail.

Whatever steps – restricting credit, raising the interest rates and so on – are taken to cure such balance of payments crises will simultaneously cure inflation. In the long run a policy which restrains inflation will have a beneficial effect on the position of sterling, but in most crises the onset is so rapid that the process, so to speak, starts at the other end: the immediate measures are intended to protect sterling and the balance of payments situation, and only incidentally strike at the inflationary situation. Because of the urgency with which a crisis appears, the measures, while curing inflation, may have an indiscriminate effect on the economy and upset investment in the private and public sector. This 'stop' (i.e. a drastic cut in capital investment) may be followed by 'go' (i.e. a resumption of investment once the crisis is past); but the effects of 'stop–go' and the uncertainty it produces have a profoundly disturbing effect on the growth of the economy.

The postwar policy of successive British governments has been to put a high level of investment and government expenditure first, before an unassailable pound sterling, and to reverse the policy only when a sterling crisis has occurred. This is in many respects the opposite priority from the 1920s, when a deflationary policy to maintain the value of sterling was pursued at the expense of accepting a high level of unemployment and a slow rate of growth. The postwar policy probably has the priorities right, but the frequency of sterling crises has seriously limited the success of the policy of a high level of investment. The relatively slow rate of growth of the British economy compared with many of its continental rivals since the end of the war has, in part at least, been the result of the frequent interruptions to investment which the crises and the remedial actions have occasioned – the crises which have proved to be the price of maintaining Britain's role as a world banker, and sterling as an international currency.

Chapter 2 deals in rather more detail with some of the occasions in the postwar world when Britain has had to choose between full employment and a satisfactory balance of payments. For the moment our main concern is to note the existence of the problem and the resulting need sometimes to make a choice. The methods of controlling the economy to produce the desired alternative by monetary and fiscal restrictions are not ideal; but they do have the merit that they treat the problems of achieving surplus on the balance of trade and payments and of maintaining a high level of employment as two separate and possibly distinct issues, and not always and inevitably as alternative choices.

This particular problem of reconciling a possible conflict of domestic and external aims can be difficult enough. In a limited degree the choice is that of the nation concerned. The implications, however, go a good deal further. A decision to opt for full employment at the expense of the balance of payments situation presumably means increased demands for imports, and so increased demands for another country's exports. The exporting country's point of view has not apparently entered into the calculations of the government which made the choice, but the results may not be negligible. The second country's increased exports may be a cause of satisfaction to it – increased exports generally are. But if the second country is suffering from potential inflation, an increase in its exports may be just enough to start off the inflationary process there.

If the first country decides to tighten its belt, to introduce a 'stop' phase, then the repercussions are felt by the second country in the form of falling exports, with the various possibilities this implies.

The consequences of a British decision to 'stop' or 'go' are clearly of interest to many others besides the British. But how often does it cause any concern to the man in the street that his country's decision to squeeze or to stimulate investment is going to affect so many others? Conversely, how often does he reflect that a particular crisis experienced in Britain may be the indirect consequence of a decision taken by a government on the other side of the globe with no feeling of ill will towards the British, but concerned primarily with its own interests? One of the more frightening aspects of international economics is the frequency with which governments, in taking action on a purely domestic situation, may hurt a weaker economy elsewhere, not through ill will, but through ignorance or indifference.

The rules of good behaviour in the international economy

It is obvious that in the modern world no nation can resolve its economic problems on its own without considering the effects of its policies on other nations. To expect national policies to be subordinated to the global good is of course a counsel of perfection. All that can be hoped for is a degree of mutual understanding, so that conflicting interests will, if possible, be reconciled. The 1930s showed the disastrous effects of allowing the law of the jungle to prevail – that 'beggar my neighbour' impasse which was resolved only by the coming of the Second World War.

Thus far we have alluded to the problem of reconciling full employment and a satisfactory balance of payments mainly as an exercise in balancing British domestic and foreign objectives; we have seen incidentally that even here there are problems for other nations. Let us explore further the relationship between the level of employment and the balance of payments, and in the process discover what happens in real life when several nations are involved who may or may not choose to take account of each other's interests.

There are four main combinations of such problems which may affect a country.

The first of these is a situation of over-full employment, of inflation indeed, with an adverse balance of payments. This is the type of problem with which the United Kingdom has been painfully familiar since the end of the war. Action to cure one problem tends to cure the other too; a credit squeeze, a higher rate of interest, will restrict further growth of national income beyond the point of full employment, may at the same time promote conditions for an increase in exports, and may incidentally attract short-term foreign funds.

This correction of the over-employment and the imbalance of payments will of course have effects elsewhere. The fact that the corrective action will possibly reduce imports and increase exports may create some difficulties abroad, for there is unfortunately no real guarantee that the correction will be at the expense of a country with a balance of payments surplus. But as a method of correcting difficulties a gentle credit squeeze may be a better answer than any form of import restriction which, while leaving the problem of over-employment unresolved, causes injury elsewhere and invites reprisals.

A second possible situation is that of over-full employment together with a favourable balance of payments. For the nation concerned this is a happy situation, but it may in its way be as unfavourable to the world as a whole as a nation in persistent deficit. The best example of such a situation is perhaps West Germany in the early 1960s, which was having an embarrassing success. Full employment had been achieved together with a favourable balance of trade. To contain full employment and prevent it lapping over into inflation the German Government imposed high interest rates, attracted yet more foreign funds and so the German foreign reserves grew. The situation could not of course have gone on indefinitely, but the Government had no great incentive to tackle the problem since the German economy was booming. The difficulty was that the magnet of the German interest rates attracted funds badly needed in other countries' reserves and so caused them difficulties.

How then to deal with such a situation? One of the most painless ways of tackling inflation is by using imports to mop up purchasing power, and a persistent creditor such as Germany could afford to do so, by lowering import duties. This she did.

An alternative approach, massive spending abroad or even massive grants abroad, was less enthusiastically considered by the German authorities, who took the unfortunate but entirely understandable attitude that the success of the German industrial effort should not be used as an excuse to attempt to cajole them into actions which to them made little economic sense, however desirable on political or moral grounds. The rate of Germany's lending and giving abroad was, however, increased slightly.

The final possibility was a revaluation of the currency upwards. Even to canvass the idea was to increase the embarrassment of excessive reserves since speculators had every incentive to acquire assets in Germany and so to increase the German reserves. The German authorities were reluctant to take this step, which would decrease the competitive edge in exports, but finally did so – rather inadequately. The German surplus problem has not yet been entirely solved.

The range of solutions – increased imports, loans or grants abroad, or revaluation upwards of the currencies – is considerable. But the incentives to cure the problem are not overwhelming. To remedy such a situation is an act of goodwill towards other nations. There appears to be no great need to defend one's own economy, for the real problem which is created by a persistent creditor is that somewhere else in consequence there will be a nation or nations who are persistent debtors, and who cannot cure the problems this creates.

A third possible combination of problems is that of unemployment together with an adverse balance of payments. In some respects this is the most intractable situation of the four, for action to cure one malady may worsen the other. A low rate of interest might help to encourage further investment and so remedy unemployment. But at the same time the low rate of interest will encourage the investment of funds out of the country and so worsen the balance of payments problem. A high rate of interest is likely to worsen the unemployment while curing the balance of payments problem.

The best recent example of this situation is perhaps the American experience in the early 1960s, when Germany's problems of excess demand at home, together with very large reserves, had its reflection in the American economy. Attempts to stimulate employment at home were hampered by fears of a worsening in the balance of payments situation. Ideally the Germans and others who were attracting funds from America would have lowered interest rates to discourage the flow of funds from America. The Americans could then in turn have lowered interest rates safely, and encouraged new investment. But the Germans (and to a less extent the British) feared to lower interest rates in case they stimulated inflation internally. Thus the Americans had to solve their problems more or less unaided. The situation was to a minor extent repeated in early 1964, when the prospects of a rise in the British Bank Rate provoked evident nervousness in the U.S.

Treasury which feared the results of such a move on the American situation.

There is a considerable temptation to meet this sort of problem by imposing tariffs. The local effects of this are twofold. First, by reducing the supply of imported goods it may stimulate demand for home-produced goods and so improve the employment situation. And secondly, it may cut the balance of payments deficit.

But while the effects on the problems of the initiating country are immediately beneficial it is clear that to cut imports may be to make difficulties elsewhere. The fact that reduced imports are also reduced exports for another country may mean that a 'beggar my neighbour' policy has been adopted. The trouble which arises is that any attempts to stimulate the economy may be dissipated rapidly if the immediate effect is to increase imports.

A compromise between a purely 'beggar my neighbour' policy on tariffs, and the acceptance of an increase of imports and a balance of payments crisis as the price of internal expansion is so to arrange matters that while national income rises, the import bill remains the same. This may be obtained by two methods: by a carefully calculated tariff so nicely adjusted as to permit the same level of imports; or more simply by a quota system (i.e. a rationing system whereby imports are forbidden above a certain level). These methods, it might be argued, are 'good neighbour' policies, but are not so excessively selfless as to place the national economy at the mercy of the international economic situation. Unfortunately, of course, this solution tends to be ideal rather than realistic. In the postwar years none of the major trading nations has really faced so serious a situation that it has had to contemplate drastic action to cure its own problems by transferring them to its neighbours.

The fourth possible situation is that of a nation which combines a high level of unemployment with a surplus on its balance of payments. This was the position in Britain in the 1920s, when deflation was accepted as a necessary price to pay for raising the value of sterling to the point where a return to the prewar gold standard became a possibility. This situation was perhaps exceptional in that the hardship of deflation was accepted for an end which was as much political as economic, namely the restoration of sterling to its pre-1914 eminence in world finance.

There are two methods whereby the situation might be remedied. It might be possible to increase exports still further, relying on the increased demand for exports to create more employment. Such a solution, however, is tantamount to exporting unemployment, that is, curing one country's problems by making other problems elsewhere.

The alternative is to start at the other end, and take steps – encouraging home investment, for example – to raise the level of national income and of employment. This will create fresh demands for imports and may divert some exports back into the home market. The result is that rising employment will be accompanied by a deterioration in the balance of payments – a deterioration which, however, will be acceptable in the light of the previous surplus, and is not so liable as the first course to create difficulties for other nations.

These four situations cover a great many of the possibilities in the world today, and two points emerge.

The first is that a persistent creditor nation, while under no great strain itself, creates problems for the persistent debtors unless it is prepared to make its surplus on the balance of payments freely available as loans, grants or overseas investments to other countries in difficulties. In many instances, of course, a persistent debtor nation finds itself in trouble largely because of its own inefficiency, and one should not perhaps spare undue sympathy to some of Germany's competitors because the Germans are so efficient.* But the case may be different where the debtor nation is relatively less efficient because it is technologically backward – a so-called 'developing nation'. Here for several generations the debtor may be technologically lagging, and its every effort to import technological know-how and capital equipment may be frustrated by its inability to achieve a satisfactory balance of payments. Clearly there is the strongest case for the

* The examples quoted relate to Germany in the early 1960s. By the middle 1960s the German economy was in deficit, an interesting example of how quickly an economic problem can be transformed.

technologically advanced creditor to lend or give aid freely to this type of debtor.

The second point is that since depressions as well as booms have a habit of spreading from one nation to another it is as much to other nations' as one's own national interest to have as high a level of prosperity as possible.

The international transmission of booms and depressions

Suppose a nation, like the United States, is experiencing boom conditions. Among other effects, increased prosperity is likely to cause an increase in imports, and possibly a decrease in exports. The increase in imports is of course an increase in exports elsewhere, and can cause a considerable increase in employment in another economy. This will cause a rise in income in that country which will be greater if at the same time American exports to that country have been reduced by rising prices in America. Thus, by increasing imports in one country and so exports in another, the boom will be spread. This spread of prosperity is reciprocal. A rise in American national income causes an increase in British exports, and so an increase in British national income which will cause an increase in British demands for imports from America. The increase in American exports will increase American national income and so on.

The spread of depression follows much the same pattern. The American depression of 1929 became a world depression. In the nineteenth century it was said that when France coughed, Europe sneezed: in the first half of the twentieth century, when America caught a cold, Europe developed pneumonia. The argument simply runs: a decrease in national income causes, among other effects, a decrease in imports: and so the downward spiral commences.

There are of course devices whereby the spread of prosperity may be checked, whereby the benefits of an expanding economy may be retained in the originating economy – or, even more important, the same methods may be employed in an attempt to keep back depression. These involve the use of tariffs, quotas or some form of monetary controls. They are equally negative in operation, however. Thus the use of a tariff may reduce imports and so increase the employment effect of any investment policy at home; or a quota may have the same results. But they clearly do not help to raise the level of exports or of international trade. In so far as, by their use, a nation is attempting to solve its problems by itself and at the expense if necessary of inflicting problems on other nations, it is a 'beggar my neighbour' approach. It is fortunate that there have been few serious efforts to solve national problems in this way in the postwar world, although there were many instances in the interwar years.

The reverse of this negative 'beggar my neighbour' policy may be even more objectionable. It is the process of 'dumping', selling subsidized production below cost overseas, as a method of exporting unemployment, on the argument that subsidizing such exports costs less, economically or socially, than accepting unemployment at home.

'Dumping' is of course one of those semantically loaded words which are difficult of definition and are used rather loosely. Strictly it should mean that goods are being offered for sale abroad at a price which is not only lower than on the home market, but which does not even cover the extra costs involved in producing the goods which are exported. What cannot be described as dumping is merely the ability of a foreigner to offer commodities for sale more cheaply than the home-produced article.

There has been a fair amount of such dumping at below cost in the postwar period. The main cause, however, has often been an administrative error at home, which has resulted in overproduction in a protected home market to such an extent that any price obtainable overseas is better than a total loss. There have even been rather ludicrous instances where British farm produce, such as eggs, has been sold abroad as a result of a glut of subsidized production.

Some postwar dumping of this sort may be irritating, but it is not necessarily a 'beggar my neighbour' policy, since it is likely to be a temporary expedient, which provides an unconvenanted windfall to consumers somewhere at the expense of taxpayers in the originating country. Having cheap goods dumped in this way is not always disastrous, and it need not always be resisted.

The Communist Bloc and the underdeveloped world

It may have occurred to the inquiring reader that in a chapter which purports to discuss the international economy a somewhat parochial view has been taken. The examples quoted have largely concerned countries like Britain, the United States and Germany; but they could in fact be paralleled by examples of other nations in Western Europe. Their relevance to the rest of the world, and that includes probably three quarters of the world's population, is more open to question.

There are, however, two sound reasons why a discussion of the world economy can largely be confined to a very small number of the hundred odd nations. The first is that the Communist Bloc (about one-third of the world's population) plays a comparatively small part in trade with the rest of the world, and the principles on which Communist countries trade with the rest of the world appear often to be dictated as much by politics as by economics. This is not to say that this trade is unimportant: but it is a good deal less important to the United Kingdom than one might expect, and it is in many respects unpredictable.

So far as the rest of the world, the majority living in the underdeveloped and technologically backward parts of the world, striving frantically to industrialize and catch up with the affluent West, is concerned, their role in world trade is subordinate to that of the industrial nations whether East or West: they tend to be the recipients, almost the victims, of other nations' decisions, not the originators. The problems of the underdeveloped nations will form the subject of a later chapter, but what can be said at this point is that the real bargaining power in international trade tends to lie with the developed nations. To be realistic: the shape of the world economy is dictated, very largely, by the industrial nations of the West, and Japan, not by the underdeveloped nations. So far as the United Kingdom is concerned, it is the relationship with a comparatively small number of industrial nations that is of particular consequence.

Cooperation – or the law of the jungle

Most people are aware of the relative decline in the power of the United Kingdom since the end of the war. At times indeed there is a tendency to overestimate the significance of the decline, to assume that Britain is dependent for survival on the goodwill of other nations. Certainly the massive aid furnished by other industrial nations has been of inestimable value in overcoming recent currency crises. But for the most part Britain can and does pay her way with the rest of the world. The crises we have mentioned, and will mention again, are in many respects accepted by choice, not imposed by necessity. If the United Kingdom chose, for example, not to maintain sterling's international role, then the crises might not occur, at least not in anything like so serious a degree.

Another point which must be made is that even a relatively weakened Britain is still one of the stronger and more viable economies of the world. She has an obvious interest, as has been said, in promoting a stable and ordered world economy. After all a rich country has much to lose. But if the efforts to encourage international cooperation, to make mutual consideration and cooperation in the world economy a substitute for the economic chaos which is the alternative, fail, then there is no reason to suppose that Britain would be the first to be ruined in the process. She would suffer badly, but most nations, the poorer nations, would almost certainly suffer a good deal more.

But, having said this, it is still worth repeating that, although there is an obvious incentive for any nation to avoid actions which cure its own problems by creating others elsewhere, yet, because 'beggar my neighbour' policies tend to boomerang, the United Kingdom has particular cause to espouse 'good neighbour' policies. For of all the major industrial and trading nations she is one of the most heavily dependent on international trade, and has potentially a great deal to lose from a resumption of the cut-throat 'beggar my neighbour' conditions which prevailed in the world thirty years ago as it lurched from depression into war.

Chapter 2

THE ROLE OF STERLING IN THE WORLD ECONOMY

A CONSIDERABLE source of prestige, possibly profit and certainly at times of embarrassment, to the British Government is the fact that sterling is not just the international currency used in Britain, but is simultaneously one of the international currencies used extensively throughout the world. This dual role of sterling is of crucial importance to any economic activity contemplated by a British Government. At the same time as it enables Britain to play a role in the international scene out of proportion to her size and industrial importance, it limits her freedom of action in dealing with what might at first seem to be purely internal problems.

Sterling is an international currency – or, to use the most recent parlance, a 'key' currency – by default. There is unfortunately no satisfactory international currency whereby nations may settle their accounts with one another. The nearest approach we have is the universally admired and acceptable currency, gold. Half a century ago gold fulfilled, with apparent satisfaction to all, the need for an international currency; but two world wars, inflation and the vast industrial expansion throughout the world have made it a very inadequate currency. Its role had in practice been supplemented even before the First World War by sterling, and especially since the 1930s, the patent inadequacies of the gold standard have meant that it has had to be shored up by other currencies, principally sterling, but latterly also the dollar. This chapter discusses why this situation came about, and some of its implications for the British economy.

Sterling before the First World War

By hindsight at least, the period before 1914 represents the halcyon days of British financial power. The major nations of the world operated their currencies on the gold standard – and this in practice meant the sterling standard.

In essence the gold standard system depended on two principles. The first was that bank notes could be readily exchanged for their gold equivalent. In the case of sterling, while bank notes were more commonly used, they could be exchanged at will for gold sovereigns containing the gold value of £1 sterling. The second principle was that gold could be exported at will by anyone without legal permission being required. In retrospect it appeared that the gold standard had had considerable advantages in currency stability that were lacking after the First World War. It was argued in essence that the gold standard had the virtue of keeping a balance in international trade, that it was, so to speak, a self-adjusting mechanism, which maintained a balance and avoided the currency crises which proved so common in the interwar years and after the Second World War.

Unfortunately there was one serious fault in the working of the gold standard. As a means of adjusting the balance of payments it worked too well: for an adverse balance of trade, which might otherwise have been met by a loss of gold, was in practice dealt with by monetary measures which created unemployment and lowered national income.

There is undoubtedly a problem for a country like Britain in maintaining full employment and a rising national income together with a satisfactory balance of payments. It is a commonplace that time after time since the Second World War British industrial expansion has been checked by a currency crisis. But at least it is possible, once one accepts the dilemma, to look at the twin problems of the level of employment and the balance of payments, and to decide which at any time is to be given priority. The problems have been separated. What the gold standard really ensured was that the balance of payments problem was cured always at the expense of employment, without there being any real choice. In some situations this might well have represented the tail wagging the dog.

Unfortunately, while hindsight reveals the disadvantages of the gold standard, these were not recognized at the time, either before 1914 when the gold standard was in operation, or even in the 1920s when attempts were being made to restore it.

The significance of changes in employment and national income was not realized until the 1930s, by which time the gold standard was buried for ever. The tragedy of the misinterpretation of how the gold standard really worked, of the excessive faith pinned to the efficacy of gold movements, and the ignorance of the real cost of the balancing mechanism was the reason why unemployment was accepted to an extent which would be intolerable today.

This then was the situation before the First World War: a settled international economic order, based in theory on gold but in practice on sterling, which was literally as good as gold and more conveniently transferred across the globe by telegraph. The concept of national income was almost unknown; its annual value and the level of unemployment were largely unknown because administrative machinery to measure either very accurately simply did not exist; and so the gold standard system's defects in terms of reduced national income and employment in a crisis went unrecognized.

The system, with all its obvious merits and its concealed blemishes, ended decisively in 1914, although its death was not certified officially for nearly twenty years. But the imprint of the system, with its emphasis on gold as the ultimate measure of value and medium of exchange, and its gold points, is still visible in the vastly different international system of today.

The struggle to restore the gold standard, 1919–31

The suspension of gold convertibility was one of the first steps taken by most of the belligerent countries on the outbreak of the 1914 war. The day had long since passed when a currency's acceptability depended to any serious extent on its gold backing.

Freed from the limitations of the gold connexion belligerent countries expanded their currency circulation, to help finance the war, by inflation.

The move had been intended only as a temporary wartime measure. To restore the gold standard after the war involved raising the value of sterling by eliminating the wartime inflation. During the early 1920s the British economy was subjected to a severe bout of deflation which caused something of a slump in Britain while the rest of the world enjoyed relatively happier conditions. It was anticipated that the necessary results would be achieved within a short time, but in fact it was not until 1925 that a return to the gold standard seemed possible.

Nineteen twenty-five, however, did not see a return to the pre-war system. The gold sovereign did not reappear as legal tender. But it was once again legal to purchase gold on a relatively large scale for export, and so the modified gold exchange standard had been created. Sterling was once again able to look the dollar or any other currency in the face, and the way was now clear to reasserting the supremacy of sterling as the international currency.

The cost in deflation, unemployment and virtual economic stagnation had been high. Unfortunately the full price had yet to be exacted. The omens had seemed favourable in 1925 to the rising value of sterling. But the strength of sterling which prompted the gamble of a resumption of the gold standard proved to be a temporary phenomenon. Soon the pound weakened in the inter-national markets, and it was clear that the task of maintaining its value would require a continuation of the sacrifices which had been necessary to make the gold standard again possible. Not to put too fine a point on it, sterling had been distinctly overvalued at its gold parity. The overvaluation during the next few years was probably around ten per cent, which meant that British exports were that much over-priced and imports the reverse. To maintain a reasonable balance of payments it was necessary to impose high rates of interest and to force prices downwards to the point where the exports became competitive. The policy of export competitiveness and the restriction of imports by price implied the acceptance of continued unemployment.

Thus it was that for the next few years the British economy struggled on through depression, the general strike, and yet more depression.

How long the situation would have gone on is difficult to say. The impasse was broken by the onset of the great American depression. The depression which followed the Stock Market crash of October 1929 inexorably spread through the world, and its consequences included the ruin of British hopes for the retention of the gold standard.

The successful defence of the gold parity of sterling had involved the acceptance of a lower rate of growth in Britain and a higher level of unemployment than was customary in the industrial nations of the world who were her chief rivals. Thus the depression which struck Britain was less severe than for most other nations, since the British economy had less far to fall. But as the slump removed even the competitive edge to British exports and their markets disappeared, the task of protecting an unnaturally high value of sterling became not difficult but impossible.

In 1931, after a run on gold, the United Kingdom authorities suspended the right to export gold on private account. The twelve-year experiment was over, and the day of the gold standard was gone, probably for ever. With it went the hopes of re-asserting the supremacy of sterling as the unchallenged international currency.

The emergence of the Sterling Bloc, 1931–9

Contrary to the fears of some, the abandonment of the gold standard was not disastrous to sterling's pretensions as a world currency. No single currency took the place of sterling – certainly not that feared rival, the dollar. The American economy was, if anything, even more depressed than the British; and certainly Washington, concerned to stave off what appeared to be the imminent collapse of American society, was in no mood to accept any sacrifice on the domestic scene to further the worldwide use of the dollar.

What in fact happened was that in time a number of countries, recognizing their inability readily to support their currencies by an adequate gold backing, concentrated on shoring them up by holding reserves in whatever widely acceptable foreign currency was most obtainable, and they attempted to keep the exchange ratio of their own currencies more or less fixed in relationship to whichever of the main world currencies was of most importance to their overseas trade.

The largest and most important of the currency areas to emerge after 1931 was the Sterling Bloc. This comprised most of the Empire, Middle East states under British influence, and several countries in Europe and elsewhere for whom the British market was probably the most important and who were therefore perhaps readier to hold their main foreign reserves in the form of sterling, and to attempt to hold their exchange rates steady in relation to sterling. Thus the Sterling Bloc appeared to include not only small European countries like Portugal, the Scandinavian countries, and Iceland, but even perhaps large countries outside Europe, such as the Argentine, Brazil and even Japan.

A word of warning is perhaps needed when discussing the Sterling Bloc. It began to emerge in 1931, and changed dramatically in its nature and extent at the beginning of the Second World War. It was in a sense a transient phenomenon, and scarcely consciously planned. It 'just growed'. There is a temptation to read rather more into it, looking back, than is perhaps justified. The Sterling Bloc was the ancestor of the present Sterling Area, but it did not have all the characteristics of the Sterling Area, and it would be foolish to read more into the *ad hoc* arrangements which grew up in the 1930s than was really there. Countries like the Argentine, Brazil or Japan did not consciously seek membership of the Sterling Bloc; but in so far as the exchange rate of their own currencies with sterling mattered to them perhaps more than that with other currencies, then, in that sense at least, sterling was partly taking the place of gold as the main reserve currency of these countries.

The situation was rapidly changing as the Second World War approached. Two developments were worth noting:

The first of these was a decisive movement away from the principle of free trade by the United Kingdom. She had clung forlornly to the hope that the system of tariffs which had grown up during the early part of the century could be checked. In fact, with the coming of the world depression, tariffs became a means of protection, not merely of markets, but of employment. The 'Buy American' policy and the Hitlerian concept of self-sufficiency were not so very different in aim.

The first tentative steps towards protection had been taken during the war, but in the 1920s it had still seemed a temporary phase. Now, however, in moving decisively away from free trade Britain took a significant step which in principle went a good deal further than even the high-tariff nations like Germany and the U.S.A. This was the recognition of discrimination in favour of Empire and Commonwealth countries.

At the Ottawa Conference of 1932 Imperial Preference emerged. It was a tariff system that would be operated by members of the Empire and Commonwealth so that where tariffs were imposed on imports these would be lower in respect of other members of the Commonwealth who were willing to apply the same principle. Tariffs had already been imposed, especially against manufactured goods, even from Britain, by those Empire nations which were anxious to protect and develop their own industries.

The effect of Imperial Preference was to give United Kingdom exports an advantageous position in these protected markets while in return the raw-material imports which arrived in the British market enjoyed a similar advantage. This system was not directly linked to the Sterling Bloc: Canada, for example, was outside the Sterling Bloc system, but inside the Imperial Preference arrangements, while countries like Portugal which could at the time be regarded as members of the Sterling Bloc were outside the Imperial Preference arrangement. Nevertheless the general effect of the system was to reinforce the tendency towards regionalization of trade, and discrimination; and, almost certainly, to reduce the total volume of world trade, while increasing trade between members of the system.

Imperial Preference aroused considerable resentment among the nations outside the system. The leading antagonist was the

United States, who saw in it a policy of discrimination against herself. She could scarcely object to the principle of tariffs; but to the principle of discrimination she was resolutely opposed, and much of her diplomatic and economic power before, during and after the war was directed to breaking the system. The remarkable cohesion of Imperial Preference kept it going, nevertheless, into the 1960s, although by that time it had weakened considerably and was much less relevant. Indeed it was to prove a stumbling block to the negotiations between Britain and the Common Market countries, and, as we shall see, it has even today not entirely ended its influence and life.

The second notable development just before the Second World War was the massive movement of gold from Europe to the United States. The causes of this were mixed, but basically they reflected the political uncertainty of the era. This gold inflow presented the United States with certain problems, but these were as nothing compared with those of other nations which depended on trade to acquire gold and now found it increasingly difficult to do so. With about three-quarters of the world gold reserve in American vaults, the progress towards currency blocs based on particular national currencies rather than gold was accelerated. One of the beneficiaries, possibly the greatest beneficiary, was the Sterling Bloc.

But as the Sterling Bloc was assuming a more formal shape it was decreasing in area. The imminence of the Second World War, which was so obviously going to involve the United Kingdom, led a number of nations to try and divorce their currencies from the British system, and the outbreak of war in September 1939 completed the process by which a number of the tentative members of the Sterling Bloc ended their connexion with it.

The Sterling Area, 1939–59

It is an interesting but academic problem whether, but for the war, there would have been a Sterling Area system: for the conditions under which the war had to be fought necessitated both a degree of formalization of arrangements and a willingness to endure restrictions which might otherwise have been unacceptable.

The broad effect of wartime regulations was to set up a system of exchange control and discrimination of which the most important part was the 'dollar pool', the Central Reserve into which all belligerent members of the Sterling Area paid gold and dollar earnings in exchange for British Government securities, and from which the British Government in turn made dollars available as needed by member nations. This tight control enabled the central banks of Sterling Area countries to discriminate against the scarce dollar.

The system was hardly likely to appeal to the Americans, but they had perforce to accept it. Indeed, since they were supplementing the exiguous dollar earnings of the countries concerned by making funds available under Lend Lease, they could scarcely object to wartime economies of this nature, though they were determined to end the whole discriminatory system as soon as possible after the war.

By the end of the war the British economy was in a parlous state, heavily in debt, and unable to pay its way now that Lend Lease dollars were no longer available. The only recourse seemed to be to borrow yet more dollars, and this the British Government, with some difficulty, did. In exchange for an American loan of $3·75 billion, Britain agreed, among other conditions, to end discrimination against the dollar in current transactions within one year of the ratification of the loan agreement. In the event this turned out to be by July 1947.

During 1946 and 1947 elaborate preparations were made for a return to the relatively free conditions existing before the war. The wartime Sterling Area regulations were, however, continued into peacetime by the Foreign Exchange Act of 1947; wartime debts of nearly £4,000 million were either 'frozen' or otherwise brought under control; and in July sterling became convertible on current account. Any foreigner earning sterling could if he chose convert it into dollars.

The result of the convertibility experiment was fiasco. An attempt to distinguish current and capital transactions failed, because it depended on cooperation with other central banks, who felt no great interest in examining too closely any transactions which would enable their residents to acquire dollars for sterling. Sterling alone of the major European currencies had become convertible, and as a result it became a bridge by which other European nations acquired dollars with ease. For several weeks the Central Reserves were used in an unavailing battle to save convertibility. But the reserves dwindled – and particularly the American Loan which, intended for a three-year transitional period, was almost exhausted in little over a year. After five weeks the British Government admitted defeat and the automatic right to convert current earnings into dollars was suspended. It was over eleven years before the experiment was repeated, and these eleven years saw the tentative wartime and postwar stop-gap measures harden into traditional practice.

The period which followed was not a happy time for the Sterling Area. Nineteen forty-nine brought devaluation; then the Korean war put some strain on the system. But by the early 1950s the worst effects of the war seemed to be passing for Britain.

The period of the late 1950s saw, with few exceptions, the gradual relaxation of monetary controls, but the lesson of the convertibility fiasco in 1947 was reflected in the hesitancy of the authorities to repeat the experiment.

By the end of 1958, however, in conjunction with the major European powers the United Kingdom moved towards general convertibility. This move was a *de facto* step and the right to revert to non-convertibility was retained.

Early in 1962, along with the other main European currencies sterling became unconditionally convertible on current account. The practical effect of this was negligible, but the psychological effect was important. It amounted to a declaration that the conditional convertibility of late 1958, which could have been revoked at any time, had now become irrevocable, in the sense that any retrograde movement would have required the permission of the International Monetary Fund.

The move was still a risk, but a calculated risk. The more freedom of movement there is in the international financial market, the more danger there may be of violent movements of 'hot' money, which by rapid and unpredictable flights from one financial centre to another may precipitate crises. But if the risks were greater, so also have been the defences; for in spite of the political stresses in Western Europe and the United States, cooperation between central banks in dealing with crises has been exemplary over the past few years.

The sterling balances

At the end of the Second World War Britain's indebtedness had increased dramatically. In all, the sterling balances which had been accumulated amounted by 1946 to some £3,800 million, a burden of external debt unprecedented in British history. Some seventeen years later, by 1963, the situation had, on the face of it, scarcely changed. If anything, indebtedness had increased, to £4,600 million. But the importance and composition of the debt had altered drastically. The sterling balances were still in one sense a problem, indeed a vulnerable point in the British economy. But in other respects they represented a source of confidence in the future of sterling.

Table 1 tells part of the story.

TABLE 1 *United Kingdom Sterling Balances, 1946–63* (£ million)

	1946	1950	1955	1960	1963
Sterling Area countries	2,428	2,549	2,764	2,478	2,816
Non-Sterling Area countries	1,301	934	812	1,405	1,214
Non-territorial organizations	26	577	469	549	627
Total	3,755	4,060	4,045	4,432	4,657

Source: Annual Abstract of Statistics

Several interesting points emerge from the table. Debt to the rest of the Sterling Area increased quite substantially in the 1940s, fell back by 1960, and increased dramatically subsequently. Debt to the non-Sterling Area countries fell dramatically in the 1940s and 1950s, rose temporarily in 1960 and then fell again. The sterling balances of the non-territorial organizations such as the

International Monetary Fund rose and fell during the period, but increased substantially, taking the period as a whole.

The increased balances of these Sterling Area countries to a large extent represented credits built up at the Bank of England and in government securities, in exchange for gold and 'hard' currencies earned during the boom years by commodity sales. The raw-material producers sold far more than they bought in hard-currency areas like America, and sold hard currency to the Bank of England – being content at the time to leave undisturbed much of the credit balances thus built up.

The figures in Table 1 in fact conceal an important change in the sterling balances – India and Pakistan having drawn upon about a thousand millions of sterling balances, and other members having increased their balances by as much.

This point will not be followed up at the moment, but it does suggest another which will be considered later – that while there might be a conflict of interest between the United Kingdom and the rest of the Sterling Area, it is at least equally possible that a conflict of interest could arise between other members of the Sterling Area.

So far as the non-Sterling Area was concerned the run-down of the sterling balances, as wartime balances were disposed of, indicated a return to the prewar condition. The British Government seems to have been more concerned to clear its debts with the non-Sterling Area countries than with the Sterling Area countries. At first sight this might appear to be disadvantageous to the latter, but two points must be borne in mind. First, such a policy could have been possible only if it were acceptable to the Sterling Area countries themselves – and clearly it was, by and large, for it enabled them to build up the reserves of sterling which were a prerequisite of their currencies being based on sterling (i.e. of membership of the Sterling Area), and also to hold reserves in one of the most widely acceptable international currencies. Secondly, if the United Kingdom is the banker for the Sterling Area, it is a prerequisite that the banker must borrow as well as lend.

The increase in the balances of the non-territorial organizations between 1946 and 1963 can be regarded in two lights: possibly as an embarrassment – though not an acute one, as these balances are not likely to be particularly volatile (in the sense that they could be used to speculate against sterling); but also as a reflection of sterling's importance in the sphere of international finance.

The figures in Table 1 conceal another change. In 1947 nearly half the sterling balances were blocked, i.e. they could not be fully drawn upon. This blocking, a condition of the American Loan, was necessary to prevent the collapse of sterling by a rush to convert massive wartime debts into goods or other currencies. By the mid 1950s virtually all the blocked accounts had been paid off and the balances were, in theory at least, fairly freely available. The disappearance of the machinery of blocking and tight control was, of course, absolutely necessary if sterling's claims to be an international currency were to be taken seriously. But at the same time this theoretical volatility of the balances, all 'payable on demand' as it were, could conceivably prove to be a source of grave embarrassment if there was a substantial and rapid run-down. For against the short-term liabilities that unblocked sterling balances of about £4,000 million represented, there were short-term assets, the gold and convertible currency reserves, of only some £1,000 million.

This was indeed a classic 'heads I win, tails you lose' situation for the speculator against sterling, and if the reserves were run down by a rapid conversion the 4:1 ratio of liabilities to assets would rapidly approach £3,600 million liabilities to £600 million assets, i.e. 6:1 and worse. And of course the bigger the drain the greater the danger for the remaining holders of sterling balances that they would not recover their assets if the 'run on the bank' forced the bank either to suspend dealings, by blocking the remaining balances, or to devalue.

The more speculation there was against sterling the more chance there was of success in forcing a devaluation; a thirty per cent devaluation such as occurred in 1949 (i.e. from £1 = $4·03 to £1 = $2·80) would enable the successful speculator to buy back assets of about £1·4 million where he had previously sold assets of £1 million to speculate with before devaluation

(£1 before devaluation = $4 = £1·4 after devaluation). If of course the run on sterling was checked the speculator would have lost virtually nothing, and could readily and with little loss switch back into sterling at the old rate. That a non-resident should be able to gain but not lose by speculating against sterling during a crisis, while one might lose but could not gain by refraining from such speculation, did little to stabilize the situation in any of the postwar sterling crises.

A 4:1 ratio is not in fact as dangerous as it at first appears. A large part of the sterling balances represents backing of local currencies based on sterling and is therefore not likely to be liquidated. It is of course open to any of the countries concerned to change the statutory basis of its currency: India has done so. But such a change is likely to arise from a currency crisis in the country concerned which requires the use of its last foreign currency reserves, rather than because of a sterling crisis.

Thus up to perhaps half of these balances can be regarded as being subject to some form of funding, and not therefore too volatile. The same can be said of the funds held by the non-territorial organizations, at least in the sense that these organizations exist to strengthen the standing of such international currencies as sterling, rather than to speculate against them.

Why then has the United Kingdom failed to reduce its debts in spite of the over-all success of its trading position with the rest of the world since the end of the war? It has not in practice been British policy to reduce substantially the total of these debts, but rather to use the balance of payments surplus which has been usual in almost every year since 1948 to rebuild her overseas assets. Partly this has involved loans, and partly it has involved the creation of new investments overseas.

The value of British investments overseas is difficult to assess since they would be sold only if this was unavoidable, and in such circumstances they could not, of course, realize an adequate price. But two things are certain. The first is that the value of overseas assets sold during and after the war has now been substantially surpassed, so that the value of British assets overseas is greater than ever. Moreover, in actual value the assets almost certainly exceed greatly the net liabilities of the United Kingdom. This remarkable growth of overseas investment has been at times an expensive business in more senses than one. But one of the most encouraging aspects of the whole history of the British economy since the war has been that the parlous state of indebtedness has been converted into a situation where the United Kingdom is almost certainly a net creditor when all the liabilities are compared with all the assets.

The difficulty which has not, of course, been resolved is that at least three quarters of the assets are in the form of long-term investments, while the bulk of the liabilities are, in theory if not in practice, short-term. In the event of a drain on sterling these overseas assets would be irrelevant in so far as they could not be readily realized in foreign currency with which to bolster up sterling. Thus in a sense the ratio of short-term assets to short-term liabilities has not altered greatly during the postwar years, and a series of postwar crises have been in part at least brought about by this fact.

It would have been possible, by using the surplus on the balance of payments, either to reduce the level of sterling balances or else to double or even treble the short-term assets in the form of gold or convertible currency reserve. There were, or appeared to be, cogent reasons against following either of these courses.

To reduce the size of the sterling balances would, during the 1940s and early 1950s, have meant discouraging the raw-material producers of the Outer Sterling Area from contributing gold and dollars to the Central Reserves and obtaining sterling balances in exchange, a practice which brought gold and hard currency into the Bank of England when it was most desperately needed. In the late 1950s the shortage of gold and hard currencies was not so acute as a few years earlier, and to discourage the practice then would in effect have hastened an end to the Sterling Area system, for a refusal to borrow would inevitably have meant an inability to lend; and the availability of London as a capital market for the Sterling Area is an essential part of the system's mechanism.

The alternative course – building up a large gold and convertible currency reserve – was open to the same objections. This could have been done only at the expense of overseas investments or by restricting access to the capital market.

A secondary and less publicized advantage of overseas investment, as against greater reserves, was that it offered the possibility of a fairly high return and capital appreciation, while reserves at best carry a very small return, and at worst their purchasing power is reduced by what seems almost to be a chronic state of inflation.

The deliberate decision to concentrate on building up the long-term overseas assets was thus perhaps inevitable if the Sterling Area were to remain a practical proposition. It has resulted in some distinct advantages, including the restoration of a comfortable creditor position *vis-à-vis* the rest of the world; an investment income from abroad which makes an impression on the balance of payments, and the possibility of capital appreciation. Disadvantages have been the imbalance of short-term liabilities to short-term assets, and the ever-present threat of a run on sterling, with the possibility of devaluation being forced on sterling regardless of its basic soundness. Crises have been numerous since the war (1947, 1949, 1951, 1955, 1957, 1961 and 1964 onwards); in at least half of these the weakness of sterling has been not its purchasing power, nor even Britain's balance of payments with the rest of the world, but an awareness of the vulnerable state of the assets.

Sterling crises since the war

The experience of the United Kingdom since the end of the war has been not least eventful from the point of view of maintaining sterling's role as an international currency.

In a sense the end of the war itself signalled the first of the crises. The wartime balance of payments had presented virtually no problems on two counts. First, that during the war Lend Lease ensured that all essential supplies which would normally be paid for by dollars or hard currency were in effect obtained free from the United States. Secondly, once all the major industrial markets of the world outside Britain and the United States were cut off from supplies by the allied blockade, it was relatively simple for all the raw materials that could be delivered to be obtained on credit; indeed the problem was rather to avoid accepting unnecessary supplies from the exporting countries, which were pressing their unsaleable surpluses on the United Kingdom.

The end of the war had two immediate effects. The industrial markets of continental Europe and Japan were once again open to their traditional suppliers of raw materials. While there might be temporary problems of payment, the fact remained that the raw-material-exporting countries which during the war had been relieved to dispose of their exports, even if only for credits, now had alternative markets and therefore could and did take a tougher line on payments by the United Kingdom. Moreover the cessation of hostilities meant an immediate end to Lend Lease – Britain now had to pay her way on all goods from the United States, even on those 'in the pipeline' when Lend Lease was so abruptly cut off. Thus her financial position became far more precarious when the war ended than it had ever been during hostilities. For Britain, military victory came close to being economic disaster.

The immediate crisis was met by a generous, but not over-generous, loan from the United States (and one from Canada) on interest terms which were light, but on other conditions which, as we have seen, proved impossible to fulfil.

The American Loan postponed rather than eliminated the problem. By mid July 1947, a bare year after the ratification of the Loan, the dollar resources, which had been intended to tide the British economy over three years of adjustment, were exhausted, and economic disaster again faced not only Britain but the entire continent of Europe. The crisis was once again surmounted at the eleventh hour by the open-hearted and open-handed generosity of the United States, which through the European Recovery Programme – the Marshall Plan – passed vast amounts of dollar gifts into Europe. Within a few years Europe's prospects had changed dramatically and she was firmly back on the road to prosperity.

However, for the United Kingdom, the recipient of a large

part of the American aid, the problem of sterling was not resolved. After a period of voluntary wage restraint, inflation – suppressed in its effects by rationing and fiscal controls, but still inflation – had reappeared. Rightly or wrongly the Chancellor of the Exchequer, Sir Stafford Cripps, took the line that sterling was overvalued and when speculation against it occurred again in 1949 he devalued the pound by some thirty per cent, from a par value of $4·03 to $2·80. In this devaluation the British example was followed by every other member of the Sterling Area (except Pakistan, which did not devalue till 1955) and by many other countries, whose economies were closely linked with Britain's, or whose competitive economies required a devaluation for self-defence, to prevent the cheapened British exports gaining a marked price advantage.

The massive devaluations which followed saved the United Kingdom from some embarrassing recriminations, but it was a most telling blow against sterling's claims as an international currency. What was yet more unfortunate was that even this drastic devaluation did not solve once and for all the problem of defending sterling by reducing its par value to a more realistic rate. The devaluation, in short, was largely a failure.

A number of factors contributed to this. As a means of improving a balance of payments situation, devaluation is at best a gamble. But at least two conditions must apply. Firstly, internal prices must not be allowed to rise even though an inflationary element has been created; and there must be a surplus industrial capacity which can be used to supply the increased exports which the lowering of prices is likely to create. With the economy working at almost full capacity and incipient inflation already appearing, neither of these conditions was met. What completed the failure, however, was the sudden rise in the price of raw-material imports which followed within a few months as a result of the Korean War. The only permanent effects of the devaluation thus were an incidental, if useful, repudiation of some of the real burden of overseas debts, and a general nervousness about the British Government's willingness to sacrifice its internal policies to the external requirements of sterling as an international currency.

In the meantime, however, the crisis had passed and did not reappear seriously until two years later – in the autumn of 1951. Once again the depressingly familiar signs reappeared: inflation at home, nervousness abroad, and ominous signs of speculation against sterling. The crisis coincided with the General Election of that year and the replacement of the postwar Labour Government by a Conservative one. The Conservatives had already made it clear that they favoured monetary measures, such as raising interest rates, rather than fiscal and physical controls as a means of dealing with an economic crisis. The logic of such an approach was that unemployment would be to a limited extent accepted as a remedy, or at least as an acceptable price to pay.

Whether those holders of sterling who had been in doubt were reassured by the thought that if the new government had, in the last resort, to choose between devaluation or unemployment it would choose the latter, or whether the other measures such as raising interest rates had the desired effect, it is difficult to assess. What is clear is that within a few months of the new government coming to power the crisis had disappeared.

The auspices seemed favourable for sterling in the early 1950s. So much so in fact that the British Government contemplated seriously 'a dash to convertibility' (i.e. the removal of the restrictions on current-account earnings of foreigners), and thus repeating, it was hoped with more success, the ill-fated experiment of 1947. But before this was done, it was felt that some positive encouragement from the American Government was needed, specifically in that government's attitude to tariffs. The encouragement was not forthcoming, however, and with some reluctance the plan was shelved.

In the event it was just as well. Once again the recovery of sterling had been overestimated and, following an investment boom in 1954, unmistakable signs of inflation reappeared in the economy. There was a further fall in the gold and dollar reserves – an indication of speculation against, and a run on, sterling; it was obvious that the ghost of further devaluation had not yet been

47

exorcized. The crisis was met and surmounted by a drastic cut in investment, a measure whose deflationary effects, if carried on too long, could have led to unemployment and a stagnating economy. The crisis of 1955 passed, but the melancholy lesson was being taught that the processes of 'tight money', high interest rates and deflation which were used to protect sterling were doing so at the expense of playing havoc with any sustained programme of capital investment. To protect sterling by abruptly cutting down on capital investment was rather like applying a tourniquet to a limb to check bleeding; as a temporary expedient highly efficacious, but as a long-term measure as dangerous as the original injury.

This stop–go policy was to become a regrettable characteristic of British economic policy during the next few years, with highly unsatisfactory results. The sterling crises were back apparently to the two-year cycle. Nineteen fifty-six was a good year in spite of the Suez crisis, but 1957 brought yet another, and possibly the worst crisis since devaluation. What was so alarming about this crisis was that in a sense it should never have occurred. The British balance of payments was no worse than it had been previously; indeed in many respects it was sounder than it had been since the end of the war. The crisis was in this sense irrational – a crisis of confidence – and came about only because of the high ratio of liabilities to assets, which made speculation against sterling both practical for the speculator and dangerous to sterling.

The Government's reaction sparked off a great deal of controversy. It reintroduced the 'stop' sign by a severe policy of deflation, a policy which was characterized by the raising of the Bank Rate to an unprecedented postwar high of seven per cent. It has in fact been disputed whether the Bank Rate increase was the decisive factor, but it was widely taken as an indication that the Government was willing to accept policies which, if persisted in, would bring not merely a drastic fall in capital investment but also a level of unemployment which had hitherto been regarded as electoral suicide. The policy was not in the event carried on long enough to create a very high level of unemployment, but the growth of national income during the next year or eighteen months was negligible – although it must be said that once expansion was resumed early in 1959, much of the leeway was made up.

Two hard lessons had emerged. The first was that a sterling crisis could arise even when, on the face of it, sterling was holding its own among world currencies. The second was that drastic action to protect sterling would wreak havoc on internal financial policy, and burden the United Kingdom with a slower rate of growth than most of her continental competitors.

The next few years saw a degree of unspectacular progress. By the end of 1958 the recovery of the Western European economies from the effects of war was such that it was now possible to secure a general relaxation of currency controls. The success of the temporary measures, of which the European Payments Union was the most important, and the obvious prospects of continuing success in the more permanent arrangements, led to a general movement towards free current convertibility of the Western European currencies, including sterling. Much of the elaborate machinery of control was dismantled – a sign of confidence, but yet a risky process which left many hostages to fortune.

In the immediate period following convertibility, however, it was not sterling which appeared to be threatened. Now the dollar, that bastion of the financial security of the West, was itself under some pressure. Although the British economy was not spectacularly successful, the fact that there was now speculation against the dollar meant in a sense that there was speculation in favour of sterling and other European currencies.

This dollar crisis (briefly discussed in Chapter 1), which was a total reversal of all the currency crises since the end of the war, had several interesting and encouraging consequences. However piquant it might have been for European central banks to see their erstwhile mentor and protector, the Federal Reserve, in difficulties, nevertheless the consequences of an American devaluation would have been as unfortunate for Europe as for the United States. For it was only too clear that a train of devaluations would have followed in its wake. It is of course rarely in the interest of any central bank to see another in difficulty, but in this case the central banks of Europe had an interest in preserving the parity of the dollar almost as great as that of the American authorities. The most practical way in which the central banks could and did help was to hold rather more of their reserves in the form of dollars. Instead of converting dollars into gold, as appears to have been the practice, they retained them until the immediate crisis was over.

For the moment at least, it passed. Its chief interest for the British authorities was that it diverted speculation away from sterling for the time being, and that it drove home to central banks what had always been implicitly realized, that the strength of one's own position depended on helping the central banks of other nations when they were in difficulties.

The crisis returned to the United Kingdom in 1961. Once again the depressingly familiar stop–go symptom appeared. A credit squeeze saved sterling, and the price was virtual economic stagnation for well over a year. It was not until early in 1963 that the economy began to pick up again.

There were some signs (illusory ones as it turned out) that this was the end of a chapter of crises. The failure of the Common Market negotiations (discussed in Chapter 4) had remarkably little effect on the position of sterling for the time being. The credit squeeze, while it was paid for by temporary stagnation, had at least left the British economy competitive with her neighbours and rivals, who were experiencing some of the embarrassments of inflation. The European central banks had played a considerable part in assisting the Bank of England, and there had clearly been a realization that a British devaluation would have repercussions at least as wide-scale as the devaluation of 1949 – a very important development in view of what was to happen a few years later.

For herein was a paradox. The importance of sterling as a world currency had declined during the 1950s and early 1960s. Yet in a sense it was more important than ever. The 1949 devaluation had caused virtually all the Sterling Area countries to devalue, and many of Britain's suppliers, customers and rivals outside the Area had perforce to follow suit. But the American dollar, one of the world's hardest currencies, had held aloof, and had retained its old value.

But by the 1960s, the dollar was no longer beyond suspicion. There had been whispers of a devaluation, despite the indignant denials of the American authorities. There was, moreover, a plausible argument for raising the dollar price of gold, for other reasons. This too was resisted by the American authorities, for it was but devaluation of the dollar under a different name, albeit for a different motive. President Kennedy pledged himself unequivocally to maintain the existing price of gold, and the issue was shelved, if not disposed of.

The American balance of payments has during the early 1960s remained, somewhat uneasily at times, under control. But the problem of the dollar, or to put it another way the problem of the price of gold, has not really been decisively solved.

The question, then, is: could the dollar survive unscathed if sterling were to devalue? It would be a bold man who unequivocally answered in the affirmative. The first result of the devaluation of sterling at the end of 1967 was to increase spectacularly the pressure on the dollar. Heavy American investment overseas, particularly in Europe, and the drain of the Vietnam conflict, caused a run on gold reserves which was to leave the dollar, if not as vulnerable as sterling, at least dangerously weakened.

The devaluation crisis 1964–7

The crisis in the British balance of payments which began in 1964 was in many respects unique among the postwar crises. Initially there was no sudden flight from sterling, no spectacular currency run, but instead a gradual erosion of the reserves and a mounting sense, not of a desperate situation, but of an inevitable failure of policy. The situation was complicated by the imminence of a General Election, with the Conservative Government playing down the dangers of the situation and the Labour opposition seeking to make the most of them.

In the event it was the new Labour Government which had to deal with the situation. It was to some extent a prisoner of the attitudes adopted by both the major political parties during the Election. But before discussing the measures adopted by the new Government it is as well to examine what precisely had happened.

The root of the trouble was an anticipated deficit for the year 1964 of some £800 million. The deficit was due to two factors – a large deficit of £400 million on the current trading account and a movement out of sterling on the capital account of about the same magnitude.

The deficit on the current trading account was the more serious, not merely because of its size, but also because of its nature. It reflected a marked increase in imports, not the traditional imports of food, fuel and raw materials, but of semi-manufactured and manufactured goods, the very type of product which the United Kingdom expects to export herself, rather than import. Some of the implications will be remarked upon elsewhere, and it might suffice to repeat that the nature of the imports rather than the deficit they caused was the more ominous aspect.

The causes of the capital drain are less easy to define. It partly represented a heavy outflow of investment from the United Kingdom: a single investment by Shell in Italy cost as much as £60 million. Partly it may have represented uncertainty over the prospects of a Labour government, which on the precedent of the Attlee administration might be expected to accept low interest rates and even devaluation rather than deflation and the accompanying unemployment, which a rigorous defence of sterling might require: if this were part of the cause it would take time to restore confidence in a Labour government's determination to protect the exchange rate. Partly the capital drain represented the booming conditions on the continent and the end of the immediate threat to the Italian lira, which had been under some pressure. But whatever the sum total of the causes there was little doubt that a poor showing by Britain on the current trading account was bound to cause uneasiness on the capital account, and conversely a solution of these current account troubles would have a salutary effect on the capital account.

The orthodox measures which a Conservative government might have followed would presumably have amounted to another credit squeeze. But the Labour Government, highly critical of the results of the stop–go pattern of the past few years, was scarcely in a position to use these methods even had it regarded them as acceptable. Instead, the new Government decided to impose, on a temporary basis, import levies and, to a lesser extent, export incentives.

The British Government appears to have been taken aback by the degree of resentment and criticism which the step provoked – criticism which could with some accuracy be summed up as the charge that the United Kingdom authorities were prepared to penalize their trading partners for a crisis caused by shortcomings in the British economy. The only reply which the Government could make was to reassert the essentially temporary nature of the measures.

Short-term the measures might be; but were they what the British economy needed? Unfortunately the analogy of the tourniquet is once more apposite. For while there was every prospect that the new surcharge would staunch the haemorrhage temporarily, there was no indication that the long-term effects would do very much to rectify the situation. Indeed, by once again protecting the less efficient producer from the effects of foreign competition, the surcharge would tend to delay an increase in efficiency rather than speed it; and, by its effects on prices, minor as these were likely to be for the first few months, it would encourage yet more of those wage demands which made an agreed incomes policy so difficult to achieve.

These were the negative aspects of the proposals. The positive aspects were two in number: a fairly generous system of tax relief on imported machinery to limit any restricting effects on modernization plans; and the tax-rebate incentive to exporters. But it must be said that the measures were more notable for discouraging imports than for encouraging exports.

The merits of the proposals were perhaps most marked in that they were not directed against the raw-material imports, which are both the necessary base of British output and the main source of foreign exchange of the Outer Sterling Area. The long-term situation of raw-material producers is likely to be parlous enough in the future without any further disincentives from the industrial nations.

The proposed surcharge on imports and the whole approach to dealing with the deficit on the current trade balance had so far caused controversy abroad, and at best unenthusiastic acceptance at home. Their effects on the capital side were more difficult to assess, and it was on the capital side that the events now took place which precipitated the worst crisis since 1949. The interpretation of what happened is necessarily controversial but it can be summed up as hesitancy and doubt on the part of foreign holders of sterling being translated into downright distrust, and this distrust generating something close to panic.

The events of the dramatic few weeks of the 1964 crisis were complex, and obviously much of what happened behind the doors of governments and central banks may never be known. But the broad outlines of the story can be sketched.

In the last few days of the election campaign the Labour party had made much of the danger signs to be found in the 1964 trade figures. Once they were in office the sense of urgency was heightened by the precipitancy with which the import controls were applied, and the news of the emergency November Budget. But the Budget, when it came, was at best an anti-climax, at worst an irrelevance. A rise in fuel tax, a proposed rise in income tax, a few vague warnings on taxation of companies in 1965 – this was the extent of the relevant legislation. The remainder of the Budget speech consisted of undertakings to increase pensions – a policy which, however desirable for the welfare of the worst-off sections of the British community, the pensioners, had little bearing on the incipient crisis: if anything, the extra purchasing power released would make the situation worse.

Suspicions rapidly gathered that the new Government would not sacrifice its internal policy to the exigencies of the external situation. This had been implicit in the election-campaign denunciation of the stop–go policy of the previous administration, and it was made explicit in a statement by one of the new ministers discounting the likelihood of a rise in Bank Rate as a remedy – a typically orthodox stop approach designed to cut down purchasing power. The logic of the situation was beginning to point to a devaluation threat. A botched rise in the Bank Rate to the crisis level of seven per cent, a reversal of the new Government's stand, with the appearance of panic rather than firmness, started a massive run on sterling.

A $1,000 million I.M.F. standby credit had been arranged by the outgoing Conservative Government, as a precautionary move. But the wave of selling which followed the dramatic rise in the Bank Rate was so great that it soon became clear that this standby credit would scarcely cover even the temporary accommodation afforded by the central banks, and that unless massive aid were forthcoming the combined resources of the gold and convertible currency reserves, the I.M.F. rights and 'swap' arrangements with other central banks could not stay the flood. For now those British firms which had foreign-exchange payments to make in the coming months feared that a devaluation would send their bills soaring in terms of sterling and were hurrying into the Foreign Exchange markets to secure their currencies well ahead of time, and well before devaluation. At the same time, foreigners with payments to make in sterling had every incentive to delay payment in the hope of devaluation. This 'Leads and Lags' situation, with sterling debts to foreigners being paid more quickly than foreign debts to Britain, thus setting up an embarrassing if temporary pressure, had occurred before but never probably on so massive a scale. It signalled the growing conviction, not merely among speculators, but among exporters and importers, that devaluation could not be staved off much more than a few days.

But it was staved off – for a time at least. Within two days a massive rescue operation was launched, primarily by the Bank of England and the Federal Reserve Bank of New York: a series of loan guarantees, amounting in all to $3,000 million, was obtained from the leading central banks. The huge funds now available to protect sterling stopped speculation almost dead. Devaluation was out, and the crisis had disappeared within minutes of the announcement.

Two questions remained unresolved. What was the price which

would have to be paid for the loans, and what would happen when they were withdrawn?

The year and a half which followed had the appearance of calm, if not of recovery. The short-term stop-gap credits from the central banks were replaced largely by I.M.F. borrowing – now at an all-time high of $2,400 millions, and by discreet extensions of the swap arrangements, particularly with the American authorities, who had some reason to fear that a successful attack on sterling would be in all likelihood a prelude to a similar attack on the dollar. But while the trading deficit was checked, partly as a result of the import surcharge, it was by no means eliminated. Perhaps even more worrying than this was that while the crisis had followed the usual pattern – albeit more severely than on previous occasions – recovery did not. In other words, there was no rapid rebuilding of the depleted sterling balances, as had happened in the past when traditional holders of sterling, convinced that the devaluation spectre had gone for another year or two, had been coaxed back into holding sterling securities by high interest rates.

Indeed in the autumn of 1965 another crisis came and went, in a sense without the general public being aware of the fact. The only public announcement came in the form of extended swap arrangements with the central banks, which were enough to contain the crisis.

By the end of the year, on the face of it, the crisis had gone, so much so that some repayments of the overseas debt went on, though the substantial I.M.F. loans remained. Payment for them was not due until 1969–70. Bank Rate began to come down again.

The fact that the economic weather was set fair enabled the Government to launch a General Election campaign without causing any significant worsening of the delicate situation, and get returned with a very handsome majority in March 1966.

The economic reckoning of the failure to recoup the losses of the 1964 crisis was not long delayed. The event which touched off, but only in a limited sense caused the crisis, was a crippling seamen's strike which effectively delayed and lost exports. A very rapid build-up of speculation appears to have taken the Government by surprise. Once again the swap arrangements which had been discreetly activated enabled a massive borrowing operation to begin. Another credit squeeze, and a return to the crisis seven per cent Bank Rate evidently persuaded the speculators that the Government would accept a punitive amount of economic stagnation rather than devalue.

In hindsight, particularly in view of what was to happen the following year, it can be argued that this was perhaps the last chance the Labour Government had to accomplish a more or less controlled devaluation. Their motives for failing to do so are obviously a matter of debate, but probably included a very human (and honourable) reluctance to commit yet another *volte face* so soon after an election triumph based in no small measure on a belief among the public that the sterling crisis which had figured so prominently in the 1964 Election had been overcome.

The 1966 pattern followed that of the previous year. The crisis had been stemmed, Bank Rate in time fell slightly and the swaps once again repaid, at least in part. There was no prospect of invoking any more I.M.F. aid, as the substantial loans of 1964 and 1965 were still outstanding. Once again the anticipated flow of funds back into sterling was hesitant and on a small scale; above all, perhaps, the price of the crises in terms of credit squeeze, slow growth, and relatively higher levels of unemployment began to register with the public.

In spite of the sacrifices which were being imposed on the economy, progress towards closing the trade gap was at best patchy, and arguably negligible. The import surcharge had disappeared and the rise in imports, particularly of manufactured goods, was continuing at an alarming pace.

The crisis which was to precipitate the last act in the devaluation drama was the Six Day War in the Middle East. The war was over almost before it had time to register on the foreign-exchange market, but two consequences were to have more serious effects than the immediate impact of the war. Firstly, the closing of the Suez Canal – apparently indefinitely – and a very unfortunate effect on both the cost of imports and the prospects of exports to the East; secondly, allegations of British help to Israel threatened a run on the Middle East holdings of sterling. The latter threat in fact did not materialize on any substantial scale, but the strain on the balance of trade was quickly shown up in a series of alarming monthly trade figures which suggested that any gains from over a year of rigid restraint at home had been more than wiped out by the cumulative effects of the latest Suez crisis. After virtually employing its armoury of weapons in the series of crises since 1964, the Government had little alternative but to accept defeat and devaluation.

No devaluation exercise is likely to be smooth, in the sense that devaluation had usually to be carried out in the midst of a crisis, when the very threat feeds upon itself in worsening the situation. But the November 1967 crisis was one of the unhappier of such unhappy occasions. Simultaneously the Government had stoutly to deny the possibility of such an event, while sounding out the attitude of the other central banks. If the other major trading nations were to meet devaluation of sterling with a similar devaluation of their own currencies, then nothing would have been gained. To ascertain reactions and incidentally to comply with I.M.F. provisions, the British Government had to reveal its intentions to a considerable number of interested parties, and it is a tribute to the discretion of all that no information was leaked. What appears to have prolonged the agony was a French refusal to give a definite assurance that it would not devalue also; but even here, some form of acceptable understanding was achieved. The last day of the crisis was, however, frankly disastrous when, following a somewhat evasive answer to a Parliamentary question, which did not appear to rule devaluation out entirely, several hundred millions of dollars were switched out of sterling, in a matter of hours.

The fourteen per cent devaluation of the Pound Sterling, from $2.80 to $2.40, ended the crisis for the moment, but left a number of questions to be resolved. For, though few would argue that sterling was now overvalued at its new level, confidence in sterling had been shattered perhaps irrecoverably. The prospects were that while any price advantage in exporting would be temporary the loss of confidence in sterling was likely to be a good deal more lasting. The Labour Government had bought time – time to put British economic affairs in order. After a year of uncertainty a marked improvement in the balance of payments occurred in 1969 and early 1970, only to be threatened again by renewed inflation. The 1970 Conservative Government inherited a much less immediately critical situation than did the 1964 Labour one but the chronic problem of sterling's viability as a world currency remained unsolved.

Has the Sterling Area a future?

It might be fairly said that economists concerned with the international aspects of the British economic problem are divided in their attitude to the Sterling Area. Each time an economic crisis has been provoked by the necessity to defend the value of sterling as an international currency the debate on sterling has reappeared: is it, in short, practical and desirable to maintain the Sterling Area system?

The price of maintaining it is clear: namely the need from time to time to subordinate internal policy to external necessity. To what extent the British economy is a large enough economic base to sustain Britain's role of banker is obviously debatable. Even if it is possible, is it desirable to try to sustain it? In attempting an answer, it is necessary to remember that the Sterling Area involves not merely the United Kingdom, but many other nations also, and that what may be economic good sense for one country might be seen in another light elsewhere.

The United Kingdom viewpoint

Much of the argument relating to the maintenance of the Sterling Area is inextricably bound up with questions of prestige, and the preservation of the concept of the Commonwealth. But the fact that such arguments are not in practice economically based does not mean that they are irrelevant and unrealistic.

More practical is the argument that the use of sterling as an international currency brings a good deal of financial transactions within the scope of the British banking system and the various financial institutions of the London capital market. The strength of such an argument depends of course on having a reliable estimate of the amounts of such 'invisible' earnings. Unfortunately it is almost impossible to make a firm estimate, and figures have varied between £20 million and £200 million a year. The question here is of course whether foreigners use British financial institutions because sterling is an international currency or because it is a strong currency.

A number of the arguments in favour of the Sterling Area which applied during the era of extensive non-convertibility and currency restrictions, and which centred on the fact that the system at least created an oasis of relative freedom from currency controls have now become irrelevant. So too have the arguments that the pooling of dollars and hard currencies made more trade possible than if every separate nation of the area felt obliged to maintain its own reserves. But it is still a valid argument that the rest of the Sterling Area in a sense strengthens the British economy when the terms of trade move against Britain, and that in turn the British economy helps to sustain raw-material producers when the process is reversed. In such a discussion it is worth remembering that the Sterling Area system may mean different things at different times.

The Sterling Area system tends perhaps to be taken for granted by the British public, if indeed they ever think about it at all. It is only when the disadvantages appear in the form of yet another sterling crisis with its attendant inconveniences that the real cost of the system to the British economy is seriously contemplated.

These disadvantages are implicit in the numerous sterling crises since the end of the war, with their dislocation of the internal policies of successive governments, the depressing stop–go cycle, and the relatively low rate of growth which has characterized the British economy for so long. The number of these crises has given rise to the suspicion that the fundamental weakness of Britain's role as banker to the Sterling Area is that not only the reserves but also the whole economic base are inadequate for that role, in that the British economy, although large compared with most, may yet be too small to provide an appropriate source of strength for the tasks an international banker must undertake.

Finally, it may be that the whole question of whether or not the United Kingdom should attempt to carry out her role is in a sense unrealistic, for there may in the short run be no choice. Britain has massive short-term liabilities; these in turn are assets to other members of the Sterling Area, and this is a natural disposition of assets so far as these countries are concerned. Whether they would for long be prepared to leave large quantities of short-term assets in this form if the Sterling Area system broke up is an open question. It is one thing to lend to a banker, and quite another to lend to a banker who has announced his intention to retire from business.

The rest of the Sterling Area

In assessing the value of the Sterling Area to its members other than the United Kingdom it is important to remember that we are in fact dealing with many nations and territories, at various stages of development and with varying problems. To assess the value or disadvantages of membership to this group as a whole is of very limited relevance.

One point may be made, however. The various dependencies, as they pass into independence and thus gain complete control of their own Currency Boards, have shown no great readiness to break with the Sterling Area. For most of these newly independent countries the transformation of humble Currency Boards into central banks is regarded as one of the symbols of independence: yet once the transformation is completed these central banks, with possibly some minor reservations, continue their membership of the Sterling Area.

The basic advantage is probably simply that of belonging to a club whose rules are not particularly onerous, but membership of which carries some useful benefits. Not least of these is easier access to the London capital market (although the ability of this market to meet all the demands made upon it is at times suspect), and the possibility that in a real crisis an application for financial aid will be more sympathetically reviewed in London. The newly developing countries of the Sterling Area have a remarkably good record of preserving the par value of the local currencies, in some contrast to that of other developing countries. In general, as has been suggested, the advantage of membership is proved in a negative way by the comparatively few examples of countries leaving when this becomes a practical political alternative. Those countries which have withdrawn since the end of the war – Egypt, Iraq and Israel (Palestine) – did so for political rather than economic motives, and it would be idle to pretend that their economic and currency problems were in any way eased by the decision; almost certainly they were worsened.

There are, nevertheless, disadvantages. The most important of these is probably psychological – the feeling that the Bank of England is, as it were, a super-central bank holding the reins of the others. It is not without significance that central banks of newly emerging countries (Pakistan and Ceylon started the trend in the late 1940s) insist that a certain, even token, amount of their currency reserves should be in the form of gold, which reluctantly or otherwise has been sold to them from the Central Reserves. There is also some evidence of an increased tendency for central banks to hold back some gold and dollar earnings instead of paying these into the Central Reserves in exchange for sterling balances. Thus a second reserve is built up – the main one, of course, being the United Kingdom gold and convertible currency reserves, to which they have free access.

A second significant development along these lines has been a tendency for new legislation enabling central banks to hold, as currency backing, securities other than British Treasury and local bonds. It is unlikely that there will in practice be much change in the holdings, since members of the Sterling Area will probably find sterling securities easier to acquire than any others. Nevertheless this is at least a symptom of a loosening of the bonds of the Sterling Area system. It is clear once again that the disadvantages of the system and the reactions to it are as much emotional as economic.

One further disadvantage may be noted: during the period of non-convertibility, when there was an acute shortage of dollars and other hard currency, the role of the Central Reserves as a dollar pool was of crucial significance. Unfortunately figures were never published to indicate which nations were net contributors to the dollar pool, and which were net drawers. What is certain is that the Outer Sterling Area countries who built up considerable sterling reserves during this period built them up in part by their gold and dollar contributions. Thus the United Kingdom obviously benefited in a period when her own dollar-earning capacity was low. But it is also fairly certain that countries like India and Pakistan were considerable beneficiaries and were able to draw upon much of their accumulated wartime balances of sterling in the form of the dollar earnings of the Outer Sterling Area. It is perhaps a provoking thought that much of the industrialization of India and Pakistan, based upon the liquidation of these sterling assets, represented a form of exploitation of the remaining colonies on behalf of these countries.

It was perhaps fortunate for the future of the Sterling Area, firstly, that the ambitious industrialization plans of the newly emerging nations led them in time to consider sterling almost as hard as the dollar and as much to be rationed, and, second, that non-convertibility ended at a time when they might have been on the point of drawing rather more extensively on the dollar pool than they had done. For if these countries, having made very substantial contributions to the dollar reserves of the Area, had found, when their turn came to reverse the process and draw substantially upon the reserves, that they were in fact being severely rationed, then the prospects of their continued membership of the Area would have been remote. This was perhaps a gamble that succeeded; but it was a gamble, and the interests of India and Pakistan appeared to have been put well before those of the remaining British dependencies in the late 1940s and early 1950s.

A further disadvantage, although it is to be hoped an improbable one, is the treatment that Sterling Area countries could expect in the event of devaluation. The events of the 1949 devaluation were by no means reassuring. Almost automatically the other members of the Sterling Area except Pakistan devalued as soon as the British decision was taken: were they wise to do so?

It can be suggested from hindsight that some of the raw-material producers would have done better not to have devalued, in view of the subsequent rise in raw-material prices at the outbreak of the Korean war. It is only fair to say, however, that the rise was not to be foreseen at the time – certainly Pakistan's decision, taken in the light of her quarrel with India rather than on economic grounds, proved profitable for the while and possibly gave a *post hoc* economic justification for a non-economic decision. But it must be faced that some Sterling Area territories had little say in the matter – their Currency Boards followed the Bank of England's lead automatically.

One of the least publicized aspects of sterling devaluation was the matter of compensation. Some creditor nations received compensation, based generally on a gold or exchange-rate guarantee, either written into some financial agreements in the postwar years or tacitly assumed. The main beneficiaries were South American countries, whose treatment was fairly generous. Sterling Area countries obtained no compensation, and this gave rise to such anomalies as the payment of compensation to one oil producer of the Middle East, Iran, but not to its neighbour, Iraq, at the time a member of the Sterling Area.

Finally it must perhaps be emphasized that the Sterling Area system is a very loose-knit arrangement. It has its rules, but it sometimes appears that the rules may differ from one nation to another. Remarkably little is published by the governments and the central banks concerned on the extent to which nations follow the 'rules of the game'. It is abundantly clear, however, that the degree of control that the Bank of England has over the central banks of other nations is now negligible, and that a breach of the spirit of the rules is not likely to give rise to any serious sanctions against the offender.

While the 1967 devaluation did not immediately wreck the Sterling Area, the fact that important members, such as Australia and South Africa, did not devalue in line with Britain, as they did in 1949, showed how weakened the system had become.

The Sterling Area system gave a measure of protection to the smaller nations in the 1930s and it was a source of strength to

Britain during the war and the immediate postwar years. It functioned at its best in a period of currency controls, for it was simultaneously an instrument of restriction and discrimination against the dollar and the means whereby a substantial portion of world trade could be kept comparatively free of restrictions. But the Sterling Area grew out of failure – out of the failure to re-establish a gold standard in the interwar years, and make sterling once again 'as good as gold'. It was a second-best choice which might have proved a transient phenomenon but for the onset of the Second World War. In its time, it gave strength to its members; and in the process it created strains, not merely between Britain and the other members of the Area, but also implicitly among members themselves. The resumption of convertibility made much of its function irrelevant, and the comparative smoothness of its working may represent merely the fact that in part it has become more a habit of mutual cooperation than a tightly knit entity. The suggestions put forward during the period of discrimination and non-convertibility for a tightening and closer definition of the rules and obligations of membership are unlikely ever to be put into effect. Partly this is a recognition of the weakness of the system, in that any attempt to impose tight control would cause a substantial exodus of members. But it may be that this weakness is also a sign of strength. The Sterling Bloc of prewar days, the wartime era, the era of non-convertibility and the last period, from 1959, of convertibility almost on prewar lines have illustrated that the Sterling Area concept is a dynamic one, with the power to adapt. It may be that the Sterling Area will become increasingly irrelevant, acceptable to all because it has few, if any, positive disadvantages, and thus survive for a time by sheer inertia. But it is at least as likely that the system will prove one of those bridges which are so badly needed to link the ambitions and requirements of the raw-material producers with those of the great industrial nations. If Britain eventually becomes a member of the Common Market, or perhaps even of an Atlantic Community of free trade under a common currency, then the greatest days of the Sterling Area system may lie ahead, and not in the past.

The value of the pound sterling

At the end of the Second World War, the value of sterling had depreciated considerably. The pound could buy far less at home or abroad than in the 1930s. When Britain joined the International Monetary Fund the pound was defined as having a value of $4·03 or its equivalent in gold. This par value of $4·03 was subsequently changed in 1949 to £1 = $2·80, and in 1967 to $2·40.

Is the pound worth $2·40? And if so why? The official answer is of course that this is the par value which Britain as a member of the International Monetary Fund is pledged to maintain. But presumably this exchange rate must have some relation to the reality of purchasing power of the pound and the dollar. Will £1 in fact buy the same quantity of goods and services in the United Kingdom as $2·40 does in the United States? This parity of purchasing power between currencies and its effects on exchange rates clearly has considerable consequences for the stability of the international trading mechanism; and of course for the Sterling Area.

In the days of the gold standard there were no great problems of relative purchasing power. Convertibility into gold ensured that there could be no great disparity in the purchasing power of gold between one country and another, and any tendency otherwise was likely to be amended by changes in employment and income levels.

The problem became more than theoretical after the First World War, with most European countries off the gold standard and a varying incidence of inflation knocking awry the prewar relationships between the currencies. It was this situation that led to the formalization of the relationship which was known to exist between prices and exchange rates in the Purchasing Power Parity theory, which in essence related the exchange rates to the quantities of goods which could be bought. If in fact £1 bought the same quantity of goods and services as X Francs, then the exchange rate would be £1 = X Francs.

The theory, formulated by a Swedish economist, Gustav Cassell, was subjected at the time, and since, to a good deal of criticism, but in its original context it had considerable validity. The most important single assumption made by the theory in its crude form was that goods and services could be regarded as equally valued in all countries. In a sense the theory was attempting to substitute goods and services in everyday use for gold.

But are the same goods and services equally valued in all countries? The original theory was derived from European experience, from the lessons of the wartime inflations. In some senses, even in 1919, Europe was an economic and cultural entity. That there were differences of taste between one European country and another was undeniable; even so small an area as Europe contained considerable variations in climate, culture and standards of living. By and large, however, what was well esteemed in one European country was well esteemed in another, although the order of preferences might differ.

If, however, one attempts to relate the price of, say, meat in Europe with rice in India, there is so wide a gap in the relative importance of the two commodities as to make the lessons drawn from the comparisons almost irrelevant. Even within a single cultural and economic region the effects of tariffs, taxation and subsidy can make any comparison rather meaningless.

To take but one example, how in practice can one compare the standards of living of the United Kingdom and the United States? If £1 = $2·40, would a £1,000 p.a. income in Britain be a higher standard than $2,400 in the U.S.A.? Would £2,000 be better or worse than $4,800? It is fairly certain that the £1,000 p.a. individual, for instance, is better off than the $2,400 man. But it would be rash to assume that the dollar was therefore overvalued. Certainly as relative salaries increased in the two countries one might find that the American exchange equivalent at some stages represented a lower, and at other stages a higher, standard of living than the British counterpart. To think in absolute over-all terms of comparing the standard of living of the two countries merely by the exchange rates is thus exceedingly dangerous.

One assumption made in this theory is that prices determine exchange rates. But it is at least equally true that exchange rates determine prices. One can see the point illustrated in the British devaluation of 1949.

Was sterling overvalued at $4·03 in 1949? The answer is frankly debatable. But even if it was, it is fairly certain that it was not overvalued to the extent of thirty per cent. The new value of $2·80 was quite clearly below any real estimate of the true purchasing power of sterling. Undoubtedly it was set at an unrealistically low rate to ensure that there would be no lingering doubts about the possibility of a further devaluation. Perhaps sterling was overvalued before devaluation: certainly it was undervalued afterwards.

What happened? Within a very short time prices had moved upwards again so that the value of the devaluation as a stimulus to the British economy was largely lost. Here the exchange rate determined the price, not vice versa. The same might be said of every other devaluation in the postwar period. The French governments of the pre-de Gaulle era devalued several times, only to see prices adjust upwards again. The 1958 French devaluation, the only de Gaulle devaluation, was a success for a few years, but by 1963 the almost inexorable price adjustments had taken place.

Have there been instances where devaluation has not caused equivalent price rises? On at least two occasions in the twentieth century the price rises have not taken place, and these exceptions are demonstrations of the rule almost as convincing as the other examples.

The first exception was the British devaluation, or rather depreciation, of 1931, when Britain went off the gold standard and sterling was allowed to find its own exchange-rate level. It had been expected that the price of imported raw materials would rise, but in fact they did not do so substantially and the losses were absorbed by Britain's overseas suppliers.

The second occasion came three years later when the Americans devalued by changing the legal value of the dollar in gold. From $20 per ounce it was increased and eventually fixed at $35 per ounce. The intention, ironically enough, had been to raise prices internally in America and so stimulate recovery, but the desired effect did not take place. Prices stayed down, and the hoped-for stimulus of rising prices did not occur.

What is the difference between these prewar devaluations and those of the postwar years? Almost certainly the answer lies in the degree of unemployment or unused capacity in the economy. If there is a close relationship between exchange rates and price levels, then the relationship is at its clearest under conditions of full employment. These conditions existed in 1919, when Cassell demonstrated a relationship between prices and exchange rates, and in the 1940s and 1950s, when it was established that the relationship worked in the opposite direction: they were not present in the early 1930s.

The Purchasing Power Parity theory was considerably modified as a result of the many criticisms, a few of which have been illustrated, that it encountered at first. Interest lapsed in the middle 1920s when the gold standard seemed to be on the way back, and the theory was left in a backwater, so to speak, where it still is. It is partially discredited, but at the same time has not been replaced by something better. Within broad limits it has validity, although as we have seen the practical difficulties of applying it are immense. In the postwar years, of course, the practice has been to approach the problem from the other end: to fix exchange rates first and then observe the effects upon prices, rather than vice versa. What postwar experience of exchange-rate fixing does seem to suggest is a one-way effect only. If the exchange rate is fixed too high, the discrepancy between the actual internal purchasing power of the currency and its external purchasing power will force a series of balance-of-payments crises or a devaluation. But if the purchasing power is fixed too low it is only too likely that there will be a rapid increase in internal prices, which will in time bring internal purchasing power down to its official external rate. Unless it is backed by a formidable series of tariffs, or massive export of grants or loans, the long-term benefits of an artificially low exchange rate tend to be transient.

This relationship between exchange rates and internal prices may be disconcerting, but it is hardly surprising. The official exchange rates between the two key currencies, the dollar and sterling, have remained unchanged for sixteen years through credit squeezes and booms in both countries, which have not always coincided. It would be remarkable indeed if the purchasing power of the two currencies had remained unaltered in spite of the different economic problems and policies of the two countries in this period. It seems eminently reasonable to suppose that the relationship £1 = \$2·80, which lasted so long, was not merely an accidental reflection of the relative purchasing power of pound and dollar, but rather illustrates the fact that the relationship has at least as much effect on prices as prices have on the relationship. In the postwar era the British economy has had to undergo a good deal of strain to keep sterling close to its official exchange rate. But the success of the effort (except in 1949 and 1967) had equally profound effects on the level of prices. Devaluation of a currency may at times seem to be the answer to a particularly acute problem of reconciling external difficulties with internal policies. But devaluation is one of those solutions which may in the long run produce as many difficulties as it eliminates.

Should sterling have been devalued?

From these last comments it might appear that the answer is 'No, never!' Perhaps a more human answer would be 'Well, hardly ever'.

Once the essential point is grasped that it is never a Gordian knot solution of an economic problem, but only a temporary expedient, devaluation as a remedy can be seen in perspective. What we are discussing, in fact, is whether it is ever worth buying time by devaluation before the inevitable ill effects appear. The answer may be simply that it depends on whether one feels that a solution to an economic problem can be foreseen.

Almost certainly, it can. There have been successful instances of devaluation, the last French devaluation in 1958 being the best example. But if a devaluation is to have any success, it must be accompanied by a considerable degree of economic and political discipline, to delay the inevitable price rises; and delay, rather than absolute prevention, of rising prices is as much as can be expected.

It is interesting to note that when a Labour Government was returned to power in October 1964, on an economic programme considerably at variance with that followed by the Conservative Government, it took considerable pains from the outset to re-assure foreign opinion that it regarded the defence of sterling as one of its first priorities. Devaluation as a remedy for British economic ills was out for the time being at least, although in the long run a failure to rectify the ills of the British economy would bring the issue to the fore again.

As we have seen, the failure of the reassurances of the Labour Government caused the worst crisis in years, and a humiliating retraction of many of the pledges made during the Election in order to secure the massive support of the central banks of the Western world. Whether devaluation will be more successful in 1967 than it was in 1949 is not a question that can easily be answered. The internal problems of the British economy could presumably be tackled by the Government. But the external events, and particularly the gold and dollar crises which had now developed, were of at least as much importance, and were almost entirely outside the control of the British Government. A success-ful follow through of the 1967 sterling devaluation was going to require not merely resolute action by Britain but a measure of good fortune in the international scene.

By 1970, when a Conservative Government was back in power, it was still a debatable point whether the resolution and good fortune of their predecessors had been enough.

Chapter 3

THE BRITISH BALANCE OF PAYMENTS

THIS chapter discusses Britain's economic standing in the world today, and, using the published balance of payments figures, it examines the state of her trade and finance in respect of the rest of the world.

There has been much argument in recent years about where Britain's trading interests lie. Should she concentrate on reinforcing her political and economic connexions with the Commonwealth by making a conscious effort to foster more trade in this direction? Or should she concentrate more of her energy on increased trade with the new economic blocs which have appeared in Europe since the mid 1950s? Is there a vast potential market awaiting British traders in the Communist Bloc?

This chapter does not attempt to give a decisive answer – no one could do that. But it does at least discuss the quantity of trade with various parts of the world, and suggests some of the problems which arise when we try to further British trade.

In the process it studies one of the most remarkable phenomena of the postwar British story, the extent to which Britain's overseas assets have been built up – and the price which has had to be paid for this.

The British balance of payments

A country's balance of payments might be likened to a company's profit-and-loss statement: Britain's balance of payments shows the state of her account with the rest of the world.

Before examining any particular year it might be useful to examine the principle upon which any such document must be based. The balance ultimately shows the flow of funds (i.e. gold and foreign currencies) into and out of Britain. Such funds may flow into the country for one of two reasons.

The first of these is that Britain has sold goods or services, and by some method is being paid for them. These sales need not be merely of goods: clearly in this context services – the hire of space on British ships or aircraft, payment of interest on loans made hitherto, even the expenditure of foreign tourists in Britain – earn foreign currency just as surely as, say, the sale of a British-made car.

The second source of funds is capital movements unconnected with everyday trade. Thus if an American firm decides to build or buy a factory in Britain, the cost of this will require a movement of American funds into Britain. The result is an increase in British holdings of gold or foreign currency, and thus the transaction will have an immediate positive effect on Britain's balance of payments in much the same way as her exports do. There is, of course, an important long-term difference. The building of the American factory clearly represents an American claim on British production and, if any of the profits subsequently made are sent back to America, this will cause a drain on British gold and foreign currency reserves. Equally if the factory is ever sold by the Americans to a British buyer then the subsequent transfer of the proceeds will cause a drain of the same nature as the original American purchase, but in the opposite direction.

The first type of transaction, the export of goods and services, represents credit items in the balance of payments; the obverse of this will be British imports, which represent a debit. The second type of transaction – a movement of capital for other motives than paying for exports and imports – will represent a credit if at the end funds are flowing into the country by reason of foreign purchases of British assets, a loan to Britain, or the purchase of a British asset abroad; and a debit if Britain buys assets abroad, repurchases foreign assets in the United Kingdom, makes or repays an overseas loan and so on.

The first group are regarded as current-account transactions. They need not balance debits and credits either individually or as a total. Thus Britain traditionally imports goods to a greater value than she exports, and has in consequence a 'trade gap', in 'visible' exports as against 'visible' imports. On the other hand the general balance on invisible items (i.e. the sale of services – insurance, banking, etc.) is an excess of invisible export earnings over invisible import expenditure. The total of visible and invisible items generally gives a total surplus on the credit side, i.e. a surplus on the Current Account.

Table 2 below illustrates the Current Account for 1963.

TABLE 2 *United Kingdom Current Account, 1963* (£ million)

U.K. Imports (f.o.b.)	£4,370
U.K. Exports (f.o.b.)	£4,287
Trade Gap	−£83
Invisible Imports	£2,297
Invisible Exports	£2,496
Invisible Surplus	+£199
Current Balance	+£116

A surplus on current account is loosely taken as a sign that a country is 'paying its way'. It is not necessarily disastrous for a country to pass through a phase when its current account is in deficit: this is normal for a developing country which needs to import on a fairly lavish scale perhaps long before its exports rise. For a mature economy such as Britain's the appearance of a persistent deficit on current account would be much more serious, suggesting as it would that in some respect the economy was not fully competitive.

Similarly there is of course no reason to assume that on the capital account, or, as it is sometimes known, the 'finance and investment account', capital movements will balance. Some countries, like Britain, are likely to be net exporters of capital, and so will incur a debit on the balance of payments, and some countries will be net importers of capital and so will incur a credit. Table 3 illustrates the situation of Britain in 1963.

A plus sign indicates that capital is flowing into the United Kingdom, either from the sale of British assets overseas or the purchase of British assets by a foreigner. In both cases they represent either a decrease in assets or an increase in liabilities. Conversely a minus sign indicates that capital is flowing out of the United Kingdom, but in the process is increasing British assets or decreasing liabilities. The fact that the official and the private investment sectors both show a net minus sign indicates the continued British build-up of overseas assets.

TABLE 3 *United Kingdom Long-term Capital Account, 1963*
(£ million)

Official Investment:	
Government Loans by U.K.	−£67
Government Loans repaid to U.K.	+£14
Government Loans repaid by U.K.	−£44
U.K. subscription to I.M.F., etc.	−£9
Others	+£1
Total official investment overseas	−£105
Private investment abroad (net)	−£329
Overseas private investment in U.K. (net)	+£279
Total private investment (net)	−£50
Balance of long-term capital	−£155

Ideally, for a nation like the United Kingdom which exports capital (and this is implicit in its role as the centre of the Sterling Area), the solution would be to accumulate a net credit on the current account which could be used on the finance and investment account to balance out the debit created by its surplus exporting of capital.

Thus in 1963:

Current-account surplus	+£116 million
Balance of long-term capital	−£155 million
i.e. a deficit of	−£39 million

It has been suggested that for comfort Britain's current surplus would have to run to about £400 million per annum to enable her to meet her capital commitments. The fact that in the postwar world this has proved to be largely an unattainable ideal illustrates the difficulties which can give rise to balance of payment crises – not so much indeed because Britain is failing to pay her way on the bread-and-butter side, the current account, but because her requirements on the finance and investment side are relatively heavy.

The figures above show that in practice the totals do not equal each other, even when the current account and the finance and investment account are taken together. Since, like any respectable balance sheet, the balance of payments always technically balances, there will be at least one more item in the balance indicating that at the end of a year Britain's total debts and assets in respect of the rest of the world will have changed. Thus the sterling balances of other countries might increase if Britain's debit items (i.e. her total imports of goods and outward capital movements) exceeded her total exports or inward capital movements. In 1963, as it happened, the balance was in part adjusted by an increase in British liabilities of £26 million. Alternatively or additionally her gold and convertible currency reserves might fall.

Reverse the suppositions and overseas sterling balances fall, and reserves rise.

The monetary movements for 1963 are shown in Table 4; as in the capital account a minus sign indicated an increase in assets or decrease in liabilities: a plus sign the reverse.

TABLE 4 *United Kingdom Monetary Movements, 1963* (£ million)

Miscellaneous capital movements	−£41
Changes in external liabilities (net):	
Sterling Area countries	+£109
Non-Sterling countries	−£16
Non-territorial organizations	+£5
Change in gold and convertible currency reserves	+£53
Balance of monetary movements	+£110

If we now compare this balance of £110 million with the deficit of £39 million on the balance of current and long-term capital transactions we find that there was a discrepancy of £71 million in the total balance of payments for 1963.

This discrepancy, which will be considered in more detail later, represents untraced movements either through trade, capital-account or monetary movements, and is normally dealt with as a balancing item to the current account and long-term capital transactions.

Thus equipped we will examine in rather more detail the record of Britain's balance of payments over a decade.

TABLE 5 *United Kingdom Balance of Payments, 1956–66* (£ million)

		1956	1957	1958	1959	1960	1961	1962	1963	1964	1965	1966
CURRENT ACCOUNT												
Visible Trade												
A	Imports (f.o.b.)	3,324	3,538	3,360	3,617	4,106	4,013	4,059	4,370	5,016	5,065	5,262
	Exports and re-exports (f.o.b.)	3,377	3,509	3,407	3,522	3,728	3,883	3,991	4,287	4,471	4,784	5,110
Total		+53	−29	+47	−95	−378	−130	−68	−83	−545	−281	−152
Invisibles												
Government												
B	Debits	264	253	281	276	336	380	404	421	477	492	503
	Credits	92	106	57	43	49	44	37	40	45	46	43
Transport												
Shipping												
C	Debits	659	652	588	619	689	696	690	688	739	750	744
	Credits	611	659	631	624	639	648	645	662	703	752	767
Civil aviation												
	Debits	45	52	59	67	79	96	66	105	117	135	152
	Credits	44	49	61	78	95	108	88	129	141	158	175
Travel												
D	Debits	132	146	154	167	188	204	214	241	261	290	297
	Credits	121	129	134	144	171	181	194	188	190	193	219
Other Services												
E	Debits	205	221	221	239	264	264	275	271	296	324	349
	Credits	385	407	410	437	465	491	490	518	568	600	625
Interest, profits and dividends												
F	Debits	360	361	411	416	452	444	455	443	490	555	569
	Credits	584	600	711	688	688	695	790	845	899	1,002	940

	1956	1957	1958	1959	1960	1961	1962	1963	1964	1965	1966
Private transfers											
Debits	109	110	97	94	96	95	99	128	154	165	183
Credits	91	90	102	99	103	108	111	114	131	131	121
G Total Invisibles											
Debits	1,774	1,795	1,811	1,878	2,104	2,179	2,203	2,297	2,534	2,711	2,797
Credits	1,928	2,040	2,106	2,113	2,210	2,275	2,345	2,496	2,677	2,882	2,890
Net	+154	+245	+295	+235	+106	+96	+142	+199	+143	+171	+93
Current Balance	+207	+216	+342	+140	−272	−34	+74	+116	−402	−110	−59
LONG-TERM CAPITAL ACCOUNT*											
Inter-government loans (net)											
H By United Kingdom government	+20	+16	+16	+28	−20	+48	−47				
To United Kingdom government	−70	+59	−60	−146	−72	−64	−44	−97	−101	−66	−62
I U.K. subscriptions to I.M.F., I.F.C., I.D.A., and European Fund	−5	—	—	−236	−10	−9	−9	—	—	—	—
Other United Kingdom official long-term capital (net)	−13	−9	−6	−2	—	−20	−5	−8	−15	−18	−19
J Private Investment											
Abroad	−258	−298	−298	−307	−313	−326	−259	−329	−406	−356	−317
In, the United Kingdom	+139	+126	+165	+176	+228	+417	+274	+279	+148	+208	282
K Balance of Long-term Capital	−187	−106	−183	−487	−187	+46	−90	−155	−374	−232	−116

	1956	1957	1958	1959	1960	1961	1962	1963	1964	1965	1966
L BALANCE OF CURRENT AND LONG-TERM CAPITAL TRANSACTIONS	+20	+110	+159	−347	−459	+12	−16	−39	−776	−342	−175
M BALANCING ITEM	+43	+97	+43	+58	+269	+8	+115	−71	+45	+104	−1
MONETARY MOVEMENTS*											
Miscellaneous capital, changes in the United Kingdom account with non-territorial organizations, etc.	−20	−172	+59	+278	+465	+10	−283	+57	+609	+484	−106
United Kingdom official holdings of non-convertible currencies	−1	−22	+23	+8	+2	+1	+1	—	—	—	—
Gold and convertible currency reserves	−42	−13	−284	+119	−177	−31	+183	+53	+122	−246	+282†
Balance of Monetary Movements	−63	−207	−202	+405	+190	−20	−99	+110	+731	+238	+176

* Assets: increase − /decrease +. Liabilities: increase +/decrease −.
† This includes a once for all conversion of dollar portfolio holdings of £316 million into the reserves.

The current account

A. Visible trade

Both imports and exports are valued f.o.b. (free on board), i.e. including all costs up to the point of loading. A valuation c.i.f. (cost, insurance, freight) would in addition have included sea-voyage costs and insurance. The method of classification is not particularly important, provided it is consistent: if, for example, exports were valued f.o.b. and imports c.i.f. for the world as a whole, one would get an odd situation where the world's imports were of greater value than its exports.

With an f.o.b. valuation, as here, the costs of insurance and freight charges will appear elsewhere in the invisible trade items.

In so far as London and other ports may have an entrepôt function, some of the imports will reappear as re-exports, e.g. tea might appear as an import, be blended and re-exported.

Both import and export figures (including re-exports) show a steady rise, and the over-all tendency has clearly been a fairly substantial trade gap. An exception was 1958, when a slight surplus of export earnings was recorded. This trade gap is not particularly serious provided it is met elsewhere in the accounts, but there is no doubt that its continued existence is a serious embarrassment to all the Government's ambitions for massive overseas development and a permanent closing of the gap.

The categories B to G are on the invisible accounts.

B. Government expenditure

A rapid survey shows that Government activities represent a considerable drain on resources. They include virtually all overseas military and political expenditure. The problem of reducing this particular drain is obviously more a political or military than an economic one. Particular political or military policies must be decided on grounds in which economic arguments are not over-riding. The figures of rising expenditure illustrate the cost of existing policies.

C. Transport

Two characteristics stand out. The first of these is the relative decline in the importance of shipping freight earnings. The sad fact is apparent that the cost of foreign shipping used by British importers and exporters now rather exceeds the earnings of British-owned shipping in the opposite direction, an indication of the decline of the Merchant Navy compared with its many competitors. One qualification should perhaps be made. Some British ships – and far more American – sail under 'flags of convenience', i.e. they may be registered for tax purposes in Liberia, Panama, or elsewhere, but in everything other than name they remain British. Any earnings of this sort remitted to the United Kingdom would therefore appear under a different heading.

Civil aviation earnings are small, but of growing importance. However, the net profit or loss of such earnings to the balance of payments will, to some extent, depend on whether the aircraft were originally purchased abroad, having thus added a debit to the visible trade account at some time – a qualification which also applies to shipping.

D. Travel

In the first few years after the war the travel allowance for British tourists abroad was exceedingly limited. Now for most practical purposes there is no legal limit on holiday expenditure abroad, which is the main constituent of the Travel account. There has been a substantial deficit on this account in the past, indicating that British tourists spend more overseas than foreign tourists spend in Britain.

The effects of this were to some extent mitigated in the 1940s and early 1950s by the fact that much of Britain's tourist earnings were in hard currencies, namely dollars, and part at least of the British tourists' expenses were in European currencies, which were relatively soft and easy to acquire at the time.

Overseas travel is one of the phenomena of the so-called affluent society. The fact that Britain spends more than she earns indicates perhaps that she reached a higher standard of living faster than most European countries. As the standard in Europe rises we may hope that while both earnings and expenditure rise in the British account, earnings may be rising faster as more and more foreign tourists arrive.

E. Other Services

This is a mixed bag of receipts, including banking services, insurance earnings (Lloyd's is still one of the greatest insurance centres of the world), royalties, and various foreign government agency spending in the United Kingdom. In all, the provision of services of this sort nets Britain a comfortable surplus.

It is sometimes argued that the maintenance of sterling as an international currency, i.e. of the Sterling Area system, is a requisite of these earnings, as indeed of the next group listed.

F. Interest, profits and dividends

The account shows that, whatever criticism may be made of the policy of maintaining a Sterling Area system, the complementary section which requires a heavy British overseas investment has given rise to a substantial investment income for the United Kingdom. At the same time the steady if unspectacular growth on the debit side shows the increasing interest which overseas firms, principally in the U.S.A., have shown in British markets. Such investments, triggered off initially by exchange controls which hindered the transfer of earnings outside Britain, has owed much in recent years to the prospect of growing markets in the Commonwealth and in Europe. The point is further illustrated by reference to the long-term capital account section.

With the exception of the minor and miscellaneous private transfers this concludes the total of all current accounts.

It will be seen from the summation (G) that Britain's record of paying her way has been steady if not spectacular. Clearly if after the Second World War an increase in British overseas assets to replace the wartime and postwar run-down were desired, or if it had seemed essential to reduce the vast burden of wartime and postwar debt, it would have been necessary to amass a considerable surplus on the current account.

The figures show that a surplus was achieved in the years after the war, although in 1960 and 1961 the trend had changed.* But the size of this surplus has been a source of difficulty. It had been estimated that an annual surplus in the region of £300 million would be required. The figure has been revised upward to £400 million to £500 million. Whether or not it will ever be achieved without a dramatic revision of economic and political priorities is rather doubtful. But when one considers the fluctuations to which this surplus has been subject, and its relatively thin margin, it is not difficult to see in it both a cause and a symptom of many balance of payment crises.

The long-term capital account

Before examining these in detail it is perhaps worth commenting on a point which may have occurred to the reader, namely that the distinction between the current and capital account is not perhaps as clear-cut as has hitherto been assumed. To increase British investment overseas is in a sense to purchase imports. The immediate effect is much the same; but the long-term effects of the two types of expenditure are very different.

The items on the capital account may be dispensed with fairly summarily.

H. Inter-government loans

As might be expected in the case of a developed country like Britain the situation is that except in crises Britain lends rather than borrows.

I. I.M.F. and long-term loans

The substantial items represent increases in quotas, particularly in 1959.

J. Private investment

The figures are self-explanatory. The balance of private investment is clearly in the direction compatible with Britain's role as

* This is also true of the crisis years 1964–7.

an exporter of capital. Nevertheless there is a comparatively high level of investment in the United Kingdom by overseas investors, some of which is a sustained investment, some of which represents spectacular take-over bids (by the American Ford Company of its British counterpart, for example, in late 1960).

K. The summation of all items in this account

There is an ideal situation in which the outflow on the capital account, representing an accumulation of assets or a decrease of liabilities, would exactly match the surplus on the current account. A surplus would indicate a lower rate of overseas investment than would theoretically be possible, a deficit would suggest that the British role in overseas investment was being sustained only at the expense of a further increase in over-all British indebtedness elsewhere. L represents the situation as it appears to have developed over the past few years – not entirely satisfactory, but on the other hand not too bad.

Unfortunately, in our examination of the current and long-term capital accounts, we have proceeded on the assumption that somehow or other the statistics on which the balance of payments has been constructed are accurate and unassailable. But we must pause and examine what these statistics really are, and how they are collected.

They are by-products of government administrative services – collected by a process which is not specifically designed to do this, but for another purpose, mainly to collect revenues. Their accuracy cannot be taken absolutely for granted.

There are several reasons for this. The first is of course that there can never be an absolutely watertight system of valuation of all transactions. When there is an elaborate system of monetary control, the figures declared may appear accurate. But there is an incentive to evade these controls by false valuation or outright evasion. When monetary restrictions are relaxed the mechanism for accurately recording transactions simply does not exist.

Quite apart from any intentional dishonesty, currency evasion, smuggling and the rest, there is ample room for inaccuracy in assessing the value of transactions. That these are on a massive scale is instanced in section M, the Balancing Item, which indicates the extent to which the traceable monetary movements differ from the known results. The size of the figures is enough to make any assessments of a particular economic policy doubtful. What worsens the situation is perhaps that this is a net figure, the part of the iceberg which shows above water.

The tendency is for figures to be corrected, although the process may take several years. Policy cannot await accuracy, which may take years to achieve, indeed may never be achieved. But it is always salutary to remember that these financial statistics can never be quite taken at face value – and that the error can run into hundreds of millions of pounds.

Monetary items

The remaining items are in a sense merely a description of how the accounts were balanced – paper transactions as much as anything else.

There are two main methods for dealing with any imbalance – either a change in the sterling balances held by other nations or by a change in the gold and convertible currency reserves.

The point which emerges from the figures is that the total of sterling liabilities and the gold and convertible currency reserves have both remained relatively constant. The net sterling liabilities amount, as a rule, to about £3,500 million, and the convertible currencies to about £1,000 million.

To attempt to reduce the amount of sterling liabilities would be to discourage lending to the Bank of England. But, as we have seen, it is a cardinal point of British economic policy to maintain this country as the centre and therefore the banker of the Sterling Area, and this means a readiness to accept loans as well as to make them. The nature of the loans made to, and by, Britain are quite different. Her liabilities consist roughly of some £1,500 million on current and deposit accounts, about the same amount in the U.K. Treasury Bills, about £1,100 million in other British Government securities, and a very small proportion of Commercial Bills, etc. As a result the interest payable on these essentially short-term liabilities is relatively small. British assets, apart from about £800 million in overdrafts, etc., are in the form of investments at a higher rate of interest.

It would be convenient if the British Government knew rather more than it does about the motives of the holders of these sterling balances. The fact that such a very large proportion of these balances are on current and deposit accounts and in Treasury Bills would suggest, on the face of it, that they represent extremely short-term liabilities; that within ninety days (i.e. during the period of a ninety-one-day Treasury Bill), these sterling balances could disappear. In practice of course the Treasury Bills are renewed almost automatically, and while the balances are ostensibly and potentially short-term they are in practice long-term, and thus present no great problem.

Possibly as much as half of these sterling assets represent currency backing for local currencies based on sterling. There may be no very great difficulty in replacing British Government securities by other securities as currency backing. Such a course would be equivalent to a country electing to go off gold, and then using the gold backing for international trade. The Indian Reserve Bank's statutory holding of sterling has been drastically reduced as the massive wartime sterling balances have been dissipated.

But while there may be no great economic or financial necessity for many of the nations concerned to maintain a high sterling backing, the change would in all probability be relatively slow, with the Bank of England having plenty of warning. These sterling balances are in practice long-term, and are unlikely in the normal course of events to be disturbed. The point of holding them in short-term Treasury Bonds, rather than in longer-term assets, is that their capital value remains unaffected by fluctuations in interest rates, etc., which affect long-term government securities.

Apart from these sterling balances there is of course a considerable amount of Treasury Bills taken up by overseas residents and banks for a variety of purposes. Some of this investment may be caused by higher rates of interest obtainable in the United Kingdom than at home. Balances of this kind are relatively short-term and will in time be withdrawn, although presumably they will remain as long as a difference in yield, or an anticipated difference in interest yield, exists. It is this type of sterling balance which may be attracted in an emergency by raising the Bank Rate.

The most dangerous sterling balances are those that represent 'hot' money which has been transferred to the United Kingdom because of a financial crisis elsewhere. These are dangerous because they are volatile. As soon as the crisis passes the sterling balances will run down even more rapidly than they were built up.

The difficulty which arises in considering the sterling balances is that it is almost impossible to determine the motives for buying what are essentially short-term assets, but which in practice may be held virtually unaltered for many years. Thus, although in theory over £3,000 million of sterling balances are of the short-term, a considerable proportion of these is for all practical purposes of the long-term variety. In addition to these sterling balances there are, as has been remarked, about £1,100 million value of British Government securities of a rather longer-term nature – the more orthodox long-term assets.

An accurate valuation of these long-term assets is of course impossible, but they are worth at least as much as the liabilities and are immediately a good deal more profitable. Britain in fact borrows short and lends long, a profitable method if rather dangerous in a financial crisis, when loans have to be repaid much faster than assets may become available.

The gold and convertible currency reserves are of course subject to some fluctuations, but a figure of about £1,000 million seems to be regarded as adequate. It would naturally be possible to build this up to a much higher figure at the expense of a reverse movement elsewhere. It would not have been particularly difficult to double the figure over the last ten or fifteen years by reducing such items as inter-government loans (H), I.M.F. or long-term loans (I) or private investment (J) by a relatively small amount each year. In view of the repeated balance of payment crises during the period, there is a case for this. But it can be argued against it that this would have meant repudiating Britain's claim to be an international banker, and in some instances substituting for highly profitable overseas investment a sterile holding of gold or currencies. Investments may earn dividends; gold bars do not.

For most of the postwar period the size of the gold and convertible currency reserves has served as an index to the strength of sterling, for a run on sterling would cause them to dip sharply. In the 1960s, however, increasing cooperation between central banks has enabled the Bank of England, in a crisis, to obtain considerable short-term aid, in the form of loans or by other arrangements. Any run on sterling has therefore been met by such measures and the gold and currency reserves have remained relatively high. Thus the falls in the reserves in 1961 and, even more so, in 1964 were deceptively small and concealed fairly substantial runs on sterling, so that the unwary observer might form a misleadingly optimistic picture. On the other hand, if the optimism is based on the fact that the effective short-term resources available to the Bank of England are much more substantial than the gold and convertible currency reserves, it has some foundation.

A postscript – the British economy before the war

The past is sometimes cloaked in a golden glow, not least so far as the British balance of payments is concerned. The fact that after 1931 there was never a substantial balance of payments crisis of the kind that has become commonplace in postwar days leaves the impression that somehow the war destroyed Britain's position in the sphere of the international economy beyond recovery. In this connexion it is salutary to examine some of the prewar figures.

In every year, except 1935, Britain had a deficit on current account, and this had to be met by accepting increased indebtedness and the gradual liquidation of overseas assets. The war accelerated the process, but there is no doubt that the British economy would eventually have found itself in much the same position as it did in the early 1940s. The war merely brought the crisis forward by a decade or two.

This deficit, incidentally, was incurred at a time of relative depression and high unemployment, conditions which are more likely to favour the accumulation of a surplus on current account than the reverse. Such conditions are moreover in complete con-

TABLE 6 *United Kingdom Current Balance of Payments, 1931–8*
(£ million)

	Imports (f.o.b.)	Exports (f.o.b.)	Invisible exports	Current balance
1931	784	461	216	−104
1932	639	422	166	−51
1933	618	422	196	—
1934	681	460	214	−7
1935	721	536	217	+32
1936	780	520	243	−18
1937	945	606	283	−56
1938	846	562	230	−54

trast to the full employment under which the postwar surpluses were built up; a situation which, however desirable internally, made the problems of accumulating a surplus that much more difficult.

The figures of exports and imports, surpluses and deficits in the prewar period would need to be multiplied four- or fivefold to be comparable to the relevant figures in the 1960s. But if we take these eight prewar years and compare them with any equivalent period since the war it is difficult to escape the conclusion that the British economy is generally sounder in the postwar world, for all its problems and currency crises, than it was in the 1930s when the idea of a balance of payments crisis was as ludicrous as the danger of inflation.

The war inflicted enormous damage on the British economy, and on the position of sterling in the world. But because it compelled Britain to face far earlier than she might have done the basically unsound state of the prewar balance of payments, a certain amount of financial ruination has proved a salutary experience for the British economy and has left it rather healthier for having more difficulty in earning a living. One may have doubts as to the wisdom of some policies, or reservations about Britain's rate of expansion compared with other nations. But to compare her postwar record with her prewar record for the most part suggests some rejuvenation rather than a further hardening of the arteries.

The content of British trade

Britain, lacking virtually all the major raw materials save coal, lives by trade. Her only hope of making a living is as an industrial economy based on the import of food and raw materials and the export of manufactured goods. In the past this has proved an exceedingly successful approach, affording the British people a standard of living in the top ten per cent of all mankind.

It has become a byword therefore that in the postwar world any vigorous expansion of the economy is likely to create an unfavourable trade balance in the initial stages at least, since an acceleration of economic activity will involve an increased bill for raw-material imports. Such an adverse turn in the balance of trade is not by itself unduly serious provided that as the raw materials pass through the pipeline there is a corresponding increase in the flow of exportable manufactures.

One of the more ominous developments of the 1960s for British overseas trade has been the change in the content of imports from the traditional food and raw-material items, to semi-finished products and even fully manufactured goods. In part of course this may represent a lowering of tariff duties as the world moves towards freer trade. But it also suggests that the British economy is not competitive in that very sector on whose exports her livelihood depends.

Table 7 illustrates the situation.

These figures are not particularly easy to interpret, especially as the value of money changed during the period. It might, however, be said that in real terms, whereas the value of imported

TABLE 7 *External Trade of the United Kingdom, 1954-63*
(£ million)

	Imports (c.i.f.)				Manufactured Goods		Exports (f.o.b.)					
Year	Total	Food, beverages, Tobacco	Basic materials	Fuels	Further processing	Finished manufacture	Total	Chemicals	Classified by material	Machinery	Others	Re-exports
1954	3,359	1,314	1,026	329	512	167	2,650	205	767	980	152	98
1955	3,860	1,424	1,121	365	689	206	2,876	234	827	1,080	172	116
1956	3,862	1,434	1,099	414	670	234	3,143	246	894	1,230	185	143
1957	4,044	1,478	1,165	466	656	268	3,295	269	926	1,310	191	130
1958	3,748	1,489	906	439	599	304	3,176	264	833	1,356	188	142
1959	3,983	1,519	946	467	662	377	3,330	295	854	1,436	202	131
1960	4,541	1,540	1,080	480	908	517	3,554	319	896	1,532	218	142
1961	4,396	1,484	1,009	482	846	556	3,682	327	895	1,626	236	158
1962	4,487	1,570	925	533	842	601	3,791	343	899	1,661	253	157
1963	4,820	1,678	991	563	917	652	4,080	368	913	1,806	281	154

basic materials increased only slightly during the decade, the value of fuel imports almost doubled, and in the case of manufactures it more than doubled. This trend has in fact continued.

What had occurred during much of the decade was that the price of raw material imports tended to fall, while the price of manufactured exports tended to rise. This movement in the terms of trade, of import prices in relation to export prices, was thus in Britain's favour, and against the raw-material producers of the world. The volume of imports was in general increasing, but the price which had to be paid was not rising as fast. This statement needs perhaps some qualification in the case of fuel where, although prices have not been particularly high once the effect of the Suez crisis had passed, the value of imports has risen steadily as more and more industry has switched from coal- to oil-burning.

Of more concern to the British economy has been the steady rise in recent years of imports of semi-finished and finished products of the sort which the British economy ought to be producing competitively at home. It was the continuance of this trend through 1964, with imports of semi-finished products rising four times as fast as exports of the same type of commodity, which led the Labour Government to impose the fifteen per cent surcharge on imports of these and of manufactured goods. What the long-term effects of this attempt to reverse the trend will be it is difficult to say. But it is quite clear that this is a trend which cannot be allowed to go on.

The direction of British trade

In the great debate on Common Market membership for Britain *
– a debate which as it happened proved irrelevant – a good deal of heat, if not much light, was generated over the role of the Commonwealth as an alternative market for British exports.

The following tables, adapted from the Annual Abstract of Statistics and the Board of Trade Reports on Overseas Trade, show how the British economy has fared since the Common

* See Chapter 4.

Market started, and who are Britain's more important customers and suppliers. Table 8 illustrates the over-all situation between 1958 and 1963.

One or two comments should perhaps be made on the general shape of Table 8. The fact that exports have always been smaller in value than imports in part merely reflects the point made earlier, that a gap in visible trade has been the normal state of affairs for many years: provided that the invisibles follow the opposite trend the situation is not alarming. The situation is perhaps exaggerated here by the valuation c.i.f. of imports (i.e. as they enter the U.K. including all transport and insurance costs): exports on the other hand are valued f.o.b., and any exports carried in British ships would therefore in a sense add to the value of exports.

The valuation is indeed rather rough and ready – and discrepancies of a minor nature may of course be created by the rounding off of the figures. The situation is further complicated by the question of the timing of payments on imports, exports and re-exports; it is not uncommon for the U.K. monthly trade gap to vary wildly between £40 million and over £100 million within one month – the variation depending often on somewhat arbitrary measurements, rather than on any real change in the level of exporting; and we shall see that the size of export earnings tells us very little about the conditions on which they will be paid.

Bearing these qualifications in mind we may, with caution, examine in detail the picture revealed by the table.

One immediate impression is the great importance to the British economy of the Commonwealth connexion: well over one-third of imports in 1958, and still very substantial six years later. The export situation is not quite so striking but still very considerable. A point which may be made, although its significance can be overdone, is that the Commonwealth in general sells more to the United Kingdom than it buys. The same applies to the non-Commonwealth Sterling Area.

Less striking, perhaps, but of great potential importance is the relatively rapid growth of European trade during this period.

TABLE 8 *United Kingdom Annual Imports and Exports, 1958–67*
(£ million)

	Imports (c.i.f.)					Exports (f.o.b.)				
	1958	1964	1965	1966	1967	1958	1964	1965	1966	1967
Commonwealth countries	1,307	1,800	1,782	1,684	1,686	1,254	1,313	1,390	1,351	1,261
Non-Commonwealth Sterling Area	356	541	489	516	545	343	455	493	487	515
Western Europe:										
Common Market	533	941	996	1,103	1,265	461	963	980	1,045	1,041
E.F.T.A.	434	747	783	840	942	331	640	686	760	780
Other European countries	77	95	105	96	119	68	126	148	177	170
Soviet Eastern Europe	102	193	220	241	254	46	104	115	151	174
United States	351	651	674	723	812	292	674	695	652	638
Latin America	295	298	283	282	293	153	153	161	162	169
Other countries and discrepancies	293	430	432	462	525	369	137	251	457	462
Total	3,748	5,696	5,763	5,947	6,442	3,317	4,565	4,924	5,242	5,211

Indeed if we take the groups of the Common Market, the European Free Trade Area, and other European countries, we find that by the end of 1962 British exports to non-Communist Europe rivalled her exports to the whole Commonwealth, and at that time at least, trade with Europe was growing much faster than with the Commonwealth. It is this sort of situation which requires a rather close analysis of the Commonwealth connexion and tends to make nonsense of the somewhat facile assumption that the Commonwealth is an alternative market to Europe. New Zealand, for example, one of Britain's best customers, with a complementary agricultural economy scarcely in rivalry with the U.K. industrial economy, is now a less important customer than that trade rival, West Germany; and when one considers the relative populations and therefore market potentials of Germany and New Zealand, it is hard to imagine that the situation will be reversed. At the risk of oversimplification we might summarize the dilemma of trading with the Commonwealth thus: nations with a high standard of living have relatively small populations; those nations which have relatively large populations have relatively low standards of living. Europe has both high standards and large populations.

It might be profitable to examine the reasons for the growth of the European market for British exports, rather than the lack of growth elsewhere. The first comment which must be made is that Europe is a comparatively wealthy area, and the fact that national economies on the continent are in some instances similar to Britain's does not necessarily inhibit the increase in her exports. Psychologically too British business has been directed towards the European market more than ever before. The failure of the Common Market negotiations should not blind us to the very intense interest in European trade which they generated among British businessmen. The success of the British export drive to Western Europe has of course been helped by the relatively liberal attitude to trade which the Common Market has displayed in its approach to external tariffs. But this liberal attitude may be due for some revision if Gaullism becomes more than a French attitude; and there are signs that this may happen.

By 1963 and even more by 1964 a slackening off appeared in the rate of growth of exports to the Common Market. In the European Free Trade Association, of which Britain was and is a member, markets were still growing, and exports to the Commonwealth were making up some of the leeway. The causes were as usual somewhat mixed: a faltering in the Common Market's growth rate; the improving economic situation of the Commonwealth raw-material producers after a period of low prices; above all perhaps, the increasing diversion of trade as tariff walls within the Common Market disappeared, evening out towards the common external tariff. The United Kingdom is perhaps passing into that phase of checked growth in European trade, which was prophesied at the prospect of failure of the negotiations but which did not occur immediately in 1963.

How long this phase will continue is difficult to assess. But even the failure to expand Common Market trade as rapidly in 1964 as in the past few years does not prove that the Commonwealth is a substitute. The check illustrates the disadvantages of non-membership of the Common Market, not the advantages of membership of the Commonwealth.

It is not enough to find markets for British exports. It is highly desirable to find markets in nations which can pay promptly. The rapidity with which payment can be made depends not only on the wealth of the country, but on its state of development. In general it is probably true to say that Western Europe is, from this point of view, a better proposition than many Commonwealth countries, which may be short of foreign currencies and whose ability to pay depends on their ability to borrow. From the point of view of the individual merchant, who can generally secure a guarantee of payment by appropriate insurance via the Export Credit Guarantee scheme, this may not matter. But from the point of view of the national economy, a substantial sale of, say, aircraft to a Commonwealth country which depends for the payment on a loan from Britain is not such an uncovenanted blessing as a similar sale to a more prosperous country which will not expect to be lent the money. Exports need perhaps to be valued in terms of the conditions of payment as much as on their mere volume. A loan, even a 'tied loan' to meet specific payments, may not be all that helpful in building up British overseas assets; and a sale based on such a loan hardly solves any of Britain's immediate difficulties in paying her way in the world.

This is not to say that such sales, depending on credits being made available on fairly lavish terms by the British government, are a complete loss. A 'tied loan' may create employment in a particular industry and is worth while from this point of view. But to assume that any sale is better than none, even if the pre-requisite of a sale is a government loan, is dangerously to over-simplify the problem. It may well be that any substantial increase of British exports to large areas of the Commonwealth such as India and Pakistan could be achieved only by the provision of very large grants or loans by Britain – and this could be a self-defeating exercise.

Fortunately, however, this problem did not apply to Europe during the early days of the Common Market and E.F.T.A. This was indeed a boom period for Europe – a Europe which had passed the point where very high tariffs are needed to protect national industries, and which had a steadily rising standard of living. In spite of the check to the situation in 1963 and 1964, at least so far as the Common Market is concerned, which has damped down the rate of British exports, it is difficult to envisage, short of a world catastrophe, a situation where Western Europe will lose ground; and the growing prosperity there is likely to have more immediate consequences to Britain's export prospects than events in any other part of the world. It is possible to imagine a Commonwealth, with nearly a quarter of the world's population, becoming in time a very important area of trade: but it is a little difficult to see the standard of living of the majority of Commonwealth members remotely approaching Europe's before the end of the century.

Even to discuss the concept of Commonwealth or Sterling Area markets is of course an oversimplification in that it groups together a very heterogeneous group of economies. Table 9 shows the situation in rather more detail.

TABLE 9 *Imports and Exports from Commonwealth Countries, 1958–67*
(£ million)

	Imports (c.i.f.)					Exports (f.o.b.)				
	1958	1964	1965	1966	1967	1958	1964	1965	1966	1967
Ghana	23	19	17	18	24	34	34	41	31	31
Nigeria	80	88	113	112	79	66	71	73	67	59
Rhodesia-Nyasaland	68	N.A.	30	N.A.	N.A.	52	N.A.	32	N.A.	N.A.
Tanganyika }	30	22	19	23	24	46	10	11	15	14
Kenya		19	16	19	20		33	35	44	48
India	139	141	128	119	126	160	130	116	98	83
Pakistan	20	27	27	32	33	29	45	52	53	51
Malaysia	40	53	48	32	28	35	86	94	51	44
Ceylon	46	42	42	36	40	28	20	19	23	21
Hong Kong	27	81	70	81	90	31	59	66	65	62
Australia	199	251	220	160	175	235	259	283	258	256
New Zealand	161	208	208	187	186	128	118	126	128	101
Jamaica	N.A.	30	28	29	29	N.A.	24	24	24	24
Trinidad-Tobago	N.A.	36	24	22	23	N.A.	25	25	24	20
Canada	309	458	359	425	456	188	194	208	224	220
Others* and discrepancies	165	323	329	340	354	222	205	186	245	227
Total	1,307	1,800	1,782	1,684	1,686	1,254	1,313	1,391	1,351	1,261

* Includes the West Indian Federation up to 1962.

It is illuminating to examine the somewhat heterogeneous Commonwealth in some detail, for Table 9 provides some information, pleasant and unpleasant, on the role of the Commonwealth. There is clearly a good deal of identity of interest between Britain and the other Commonwealth countries: but what does emerge is that from the point of view of the British balance of payments some of the least satisfactory countries are countries like Canada, India and so on, countries which (admittedly, in the case of Canada, under an earlier government) expressed the strongest objections to British membership of the Common Market, when it appeared that this would involve the abolition of preferential treatment for their products in the British market.

Trade with the Non-Commonwealth Sterling Area

Clearly the most important single area within this group is the Middle East, for the attachment of these states to the Sterling Area may well be of crucial importance to the survival of the Area. The vast imbalance between British imports from this region and exports to them to some extent reflects the fact that there is little that can immediately and usefully be sold here. Considerable sterling balances have accumulated to these countries, and a rapid withdrawal of a substantial part of these sterling balances could have a very profound effect on the stability of the Sterling Area system. Whatever political or military inconveniences Britain's interest in this region cause, there is no doubt of her sizeable financial stake in it.

A second example of financial interests being equated with political inconveniences is the importance of the South African market. Whatever the merits may be of the United Nations' attempt to impose economic sanctions the effects on the British economy would undoubtedly be more severe than for most other countries.

It would be idle to claim that economic interests must always come first in determining British policy towards any part of the world. Clearly many decisions must depend on strategic, military or moral grounds. But it makes sense at least to consider the

TABLE 10 *United Kingdom Imports and Exports from Non-Commonwealth Sterling Area members, 1958–67* (£ million)

	Imports					Exports				
	1958	1964	1965	1966	1967	1958	1964	1965	1966	1967
Middle East Oil States	149	162	122	129	93	34	35	36	44	50
Ireland	108	179	170	186	224	108	174	186	189	196
Iceland	1	8	10	9	9	3	6	7	8	7
South Africa	90	183	181	191	220	186	239	265	241	261
Burma	7	9	6	—	—	12	—	—	—	—
Total	356	541	489	516	545	343	455	493	487	515

Burma left the Sterling Area in 1966.

economic or financial costs of any particular policy, even if the decisions eventually made are against the best economic interests of the country.

Trade with Communist countries

These figures show considerably higher export totals than do the global figures in Table 2, at least so far as Russia and the Soviet sphere in Eastern Europe are concerned. This is because the re-exporting of goods imported from this area and then sold back after some form of processing appears to be characteristic of a substantial part of trade with East Europe; proportionately more exports to East Europe seem to have their origin there than in other sectors of Britain's trade.

Nevertheless, as Table 11 shows, in spite of the substantial difference these re-exports make to the trade figures Britain still imports a good deal more from the Communist Bloc than she exports to it. Since a good deal of emphasis has been placed, probably rightly, on the potential importance of this market, it is as well to realize that the relative paucity of trade is due more to the East's unwillingness to buy British imports than vice versa. The Soviet authorities sometimes argue that this imbalance between imports and exports merely permits the purchase of commodities from other parts of the Sterling Area where the U.S.S.R. has an imbalance of trade. While this may have some validity, it nevertheless remains very much an unproven assumption that an increase in Anglo-Soviet trade would mean a substantial export surplus in this direction. The hopes of breaching the vast potential consumer market are at best speculative; certainly they derive no nourishment from the actual figures. British trade fairs in East Europe have an invariable *succès d'estime*. But they do not result in substantial sales of the consumer goods on which an increase in British exports would largely depend.

Indeed one of the more bizarre episodes of British financial policy in the 1960s may well turn out to be the massive credits granted by the British Government to the Communist Bloc. The Soviet Union, the second most powerful economy in the world,

TABLE 11 *United Kingdom Imports and Exports from Communist countries, 1958–67*
(£ million)

	Imports					Exports				
	1958	1964	1965	1966	1967	1958	1964	1965	1966	1967
Soviet Union	60	97	118	125	123	52	40	46	50	64
Poland	26	48	48	54	56	12	25	25	36	49
East Germany	3	10	12	14	12	3	6	8	16	17
Hungary	3	7	7	7	10	3	9	8	10	12
Czechoslovakia	7	17	17	20	21	5	13	15	19	15
Romania	2	9	11	15	26	2	8	19	11	10
Other East European countries	1	4	5	6	6	—	3	4	7	7
Yugoslavia	13	18	15	13	16	11	23	20	27	23
China	19	25	30	34	30	27	18	26	34	39
Total	134	237	264	288	299	115	145	161	212	236

is likely to be granted credits running possibly into hundreds of millions sterling over twelve to fifteen years, on the curious grounds that otherwise the Russians could not afford to buy capital equipment from Britain for cash, or on the short-term credits that any other industrial nation would expect. It is a little difficult not to ask whether in fact sales on such conditions are worth having, or whether the benefits to the British economy would not be far greater if the industrial products were to remain in Britain. If the Russians can afford to pay, and their export surplus suggests that they could, they are getting much the best of the bargain: if they genuinely cannot afford to pay, then the argument that next year they will somehow be able to buy consumer goods just does not hold water.

Much the same applies to that other half of the Communist world, China. No one can deny that 700 million Chinese represent a vast potential market; but as a significantly large consumer of British exports, supplied on a commercial basis on reasonable credit terms, China can be dismissed. By the end of the century it might be a sizeable market. But for the immediate future its prospects for the British exporter cannot be rated very highly.

Chapter 4

BRITAIN AND EUROPE

ONE of the most remarkable developments since the end of the Second World War has been Western Europe's climb from the abyss of destruction, despair and starvation in 1945 to a peak of relative prosperity, with the European industrial complex once again, with America and Russia, one of the three centres of world influence and industrial production. Europe is unlikely in the foreseeable future to occupy the dominant role it possessed in the nineteenth-century world. Nevertheless it would have been a bold man indeed who in 1945 prophesied that that continent would climb so rapidly back to a position of equality with the United States.

In these years, however, the history of the British economy has been less happy – not so much because it has failed to achieve much, for indeed the British rate of growth has probably been as great during this period as at any time in her history, but because the opportunities for Britain to lead Europe on the path back to prosperity were largely neglected.

Financial cooperation in Europe

In the first few years after the Second World War Western Europe was indeed in a difficult situation. Every nation which had been involved in the war was in greater or less degree engaged in a herculean task of reconstruction. The physical structure of the economy was in many instances shattered, and the financial system was in almost as bad a state. There was an urgent need for food, machinery, materials of all sorts from America or anywhere they could be obtained. But even where one European nation was in a position to supply the needs of a second, it was almost certainly unwilling to do so except for gold, dollars or alternatively for commodities which it urgently needed itself. No nation would willingly sell to another on credit, or for a foreign currency whose value was dubious: and no nation was likely to give up any of its extremely scanty supplies of gold or dollars except for dire necessities.

In practice Europe descended to a sophisticated version of that most primitive method of exchange – barter. Nations would agree with each other bilateral quotas of exchange of goods to a certain value, so that neither side had to part with gold or dollars. A nation with a trade surplus ran the risk of being paid in non-convertible, and potentially valueless, currency: a nation with a trade deficit ran the risk of being pressed to meet the deficit in a currency much harder than its own – gold or dollars. In these circumstances the dozen or so nations of Western Europe found themselves under the obligation each to attempt to fix a quota with every other nation and take steps to keep within that quota. The level of trade which this system permitted was of course only a fraction of what would have been possible had there been a multilateral clearing of accounts.

The situation, while unfortunate, did not appear to be more than temporary. Two events seemed likely to ease it. The first was the anticipated return to convertibility of the pound sterling by mid 1947 under the American Loan Agreement. This would make sterling just as desirable as the dollar and the subsequent increase in liquidity would go far to make a general relaxation of the crisis measures possible. Secondly, it was hoped that the opening of the International Monetary Fund would make it possible to meet any temporary shortages of the key currencies when the restrictions were relaxed.

When mid 1947 came round, both hopes proved illusory. The failure of sterling convertibility was accompanied by a crisis in the British economy which was but part of a European crisis. In the face of this desperate situation the existing arrangements were clearly inadequate.

The Americans saved the day by their generous and spectacularly successful Marshall Aid Plan, which pumped the desperately needed resources into the European economy, and within a matter of a few years had brought it into a state of health which far exceeded even the palmiest days of the prewar era.

It is not intended here to analyse the course of the Marshall Aid Plan – or, to give it its official title, the European Recovery Programme. In the long run its apparently transitory results proved even more enduring than the programme itself.

In brief, these results were the creation of a system of international economic institutions, intended initially to coordinate European requirements for American aid and thus, by a system of cooperation and, indeed, mutual examination of each others' requests for dollars, to ensure that there was no wasteful overlapping of demands for aid. The chief of these institutions, O.E.E.C., the Organization for European Economic Cooperation, was particularly successful, and proved to be a milestone of European cooperation. The seventeen member countries, among them traditional enemies, realized the values of cooperation, learned to appreciate each others' problems and began the process which was to turn the Europe of warring camps of the 1930s into an internationally-minded group of nations dreaming visions of unification which had been possible only transiently by military conquest in the past. The instinct for unity was by no means lessened by the threat from Eastern Europe; but what was emerging was far more than the huddling together of menaced nations.

Thus even when the *raison d'être* of the secretariat – the disbursement of American dollars – ceased, O.E.E.C. continued, coordinating the economic recovery of Europe, and encouraging liberalization of trade and tariffs among its members.

In this movement the British Government played a full, indeed a leading, part. But wholehearted adherence to the cause of European collaboration was unfortunately missing when other more specific proposals for cooperation appeared.

Of these the most important was the European Payments Union, which operated in various forms from 1950. It was essentially a stop-gap institution to achieve effective convertibility of currencies within Europe while discrimination against the dollar remained. In spite of its temporary nature, it remained in existence, subject to some modification, until general European convertibility was achieved at the end of 1958. With general convertibility it became irrelevant and was wound up.

Britain and the European Payments Union

The E.P.U. is now as dead as Queen Anne, and, in a sense, of as little immediate relevance. But the attitude of the United Kingdom authorities to E.P.U. was perhaps symptomatic of an outlook which was profoundly to affect Britain's relationship with the rest of Europe.

Sterling claimed equality with the dollar as one of the key currencies of the world. But with sterling as but one of the currencies of E.P.U., the claim sounded somewhat hollow. No one was more aware of this than the British Treasury. British membership of E.P.U. was thus a painful necessity and the British Government made no secret of its desire to strike out with sterling as a convertible currency once again. In 1953 it flirted with the idea of a return to convertibility, which would have involved leaving E.P.U., but it had reluctantly to abandon the idea. For the next few years it was increasingly anxious to see a general return to convertibility, and the end of the system.

In so far as this was a desire to end restriction of trade and discrimination in currency movements, it was admirable. But it contained an element of an attitude which was perhaps less welcome, certainly to our European neighbours: the implication that Britain was somehow not of Europe, that she was deliberately turning her back, and indeed claiming a superior status. This claim might or might not be justified but it was certainly liable to be resented by a Europe which would in the early postwar years have accepted Britain as the leading European power. Britain in short was squandering the immense assets of European goodwill, and sowing the seeds of a bitter harvest.

But this was for the future. In the 1950s the E.P.U. flourished, and along with its parent body, O.E.E.C., saw Western Europe transformed from an area verging on chaos and destitution into one of the strongest and most stable regions of the world.

When at the beginning of 1959 the E.P.U. came to an end with a general return to convertibility of the major Western European currencies including sterling, it was replaced by a new system, the European Monetary Agreement.

Partly because of the disadvantageous terms on which its facilities could be used and probably also because of other economic and political developments in Europe which overshadowed these arrangements, little use has been made of the E.M.A. facilities except by the small and marginal European powers. It is not likely to be retained beyond the mid 1960s.

The decline of O.E.E.C.

The O.E.E.C. which had originally been set up to administer Marshall Aid and was, so to speak, the sponsor of the E.P.U., survived the disappearance of its *raison d'être*, and for most of the 1950s it performed a very useful function in European cooperation in economic development. But by the late 1950s it was not actually in decay, but very much overshadowed by other developments. Before we examine these in detail, we may note that O.E.E.C. expanded in membership even as it declined in numbers. The need for economic cooperation was one that applied to the whole West, not merely to Europe; and in 1961 the old O.E.E.C. was replaced by an organization which embraced not only the original member countries but also the U.S.A. and Canada.* The new organization, the Organization for Economic Cooperation and Development (O.E.C.D.) had three main tasks: to coordinate its members' economic policies, by an annual review and mutual discussion of each member's economic situation; to coordinate aid to developing countries, a task whose importance for O.E.E.C. had increased as its other objectives had been fulfilled; and finally to supply more specialized services for its members in various economic activities.

The feeling that O.E.C.D. is a relative failure, that it has not achieved enough, is perhaps merely a reflection of the very high achievements of its predecessor. But nevertheless the relative decline of this institution in which the Western allies and Western

* Subsequently Japan and Australia joined.

neutrals cooperated is particularly unfortunate in that it emphasized the political rifts of Western Europe.

The origins of the Common Market

It is always easy in retrospect to see the lost opportunities and
bungled chances in politics; and the history of Britain's attitude
towards European economic cooperation should be reviewed,
for Britain is now paying for her mistakes and may go on paying
for them for some time yet.

Certain stock attitudes have tended to grow up in the 1960s:
that Britain would like, given the right terms, to join the Common
Market; that the French are resolutely opposed: that, in this,
they are defying the wishes of the other members; and that somehow if the Gaullist régime were replaced all would be well. The
truth is a good deal more complicated, and there are very few
blacks and whites, no villains and few heroes, in the story of
Britain's relations with Europe in the 1950s.

The whole complex has its roots in a dilemma which faced
France in the late 1940s. The dilemma was what to do about
Germany. For centuries French aggression had ravaged Germany:
since 1870 the process had been reversed, and three times in
seventy years France suffered grievously in war with Germany.
Although for the moment Germany was prostrate, and the German Government, struggling to live down the reputation of
Hitler's Reich, was markedly 'good European' and pro-French,
there was no guarantee that this state of affairs would last. Potentially Germany was far more powerful than France, and this
Germany would have to be lived with.

The problem was how to treat with Germany. The Versailles
Treaty which marked the end of the First World War had fallen
between two stools: it was harsh enough to alienate Germany,
but not harsh enough to cripple her. This time France decided,
wisely as it turned out, to try conciliation.

The French Foreign Minister of the day, Robert Schuman,
saw such an opportunity in the rebuilding of the industrial region
extending from Alsace-Lorraine in France, through Belgium and

Luxemburg, into the Ruhr Valley of Germany. If this region of coal and steel production could be rebuilt as an economic unit rather than within national frontiers it would replace national rivalry by national interdependence.

The Schuman plan thus envisaged a system where coal and steel would move freely in the area without regard to national frontiers. An essential part of such an arrangement would be that it would be run not merely by a joint committee but by a supranational authority, which would administer the Coal and Steel Community, with an International Court to consider the rules of behaviour within the Community, whose decisions would be binding.

The French proposal appealed to the pro-French Adenauer Government of West Germany. Quite apart from its excellent economic sense, this was an opportunity for West Germany, for the first time since 1945, to treat on equal terms with the other European nations. The effect of France's offering the hand of friendship and an entrée on equal terms to the nations of Europe was enormous. Germany accepted the plan.

So far, so good. But the French were well aware that, as constituted, the Community could not but be dominated by Germany, whose economy was far more advanced than that of France. To keep some sort of check on Germany it was desirable to interest as many nations as possible in the concept.

The timing was right. Western Europe, torn and exhausted by internecine wars, and once again menaced from the East, was in the mood for cooperation. To Belgium, Luxemburg and Holland, the first two part of the industrial complex, and all three countries almost inevitably involved in any Franco-German conflict, the idea was an excellent one. To Italy, almost totally lacking its own iron and coal resources, anything which made for the free movement of these commodities was advantageous, quite apart from the political ends.

Thus the nucleus grew; six nations whose destinies were to become almost inextricably mixed.

So far the only important industrial nation which had not joined was Britain. It must be emphasized that all six nations, including the French, were very anxious to have British membership. Britain was at this time the natural leader of Europe. An unstable France would have accepted a British lead, none of the others would have accepted Germany, and the smaller nations looked to Britain to counter the large ones and to give an element of stability which was badly needed.

It was the opportunity which occurs but once in a century and the British Government rejected it.

In fairness it must be said that the British Government was in some difficulties. The postwar Labour Government, on its last legs, was engaged in nationalizing steel. It had already nationalized the coal industry. Although the Community could function with a nationally owned or privately owned industry, the British Government of the time felt that the Community would negate the very principle of nationalization, namely control by the State in the interests of the national economy, and substitute in its place control by a supranational authority whose views might not coincide with those of the British Government.

Behind this objection, however, lay a far graver one. The British Government had not made up its mind whether it was the third world power, or the leading European power. Was Britain a part of Europe? So far as the question of national sovereignty was concerned, the answer was clear. Britain would not sacrifice any degree of national sovereignty.

Within a few months a Conservative Government had replaced the Labour Government and the process of steel nationalization went into reverse. But in their attitudes towards a sacrifice of national sovereignty there was no difference between Labour and Conservative. The refusal was firm.

The reaction in Europe was considerable disappointment, and even perhaps the start of that resentment which was to grow with the years. The British had begun to accumulate the reputation of being bad Europeans: the French, as originators and prime movers of the European concept, were gathering golden opinions and a reserve of goodwill which they were later to exploit successfully.

The success of the European Coal and Steel Community in the

early 1950s took even its strongest advocates by surprise. At least some of the credit may in truth have been due to an unhappy era. From 1940 to 1944, the German *Festung Europa* ('Fortress Europe') had been an economic unit. Occupied Europe had been compelled more and more to develop trade links, and even the collapse of Hitler's grandiose empire had not completely severed the commercial links forged during these four years.

In the Community, Germany was but one of six, and her heavy industry was to that extent out of national control. While the Six showed a readiness to experiment in closer economic and political cooperation the British Government remained aloof, apparently unconvinced of the importance of the developments or of the ability of the Six to work together.

For a few months in mid 1954 the British attitude seemed to be borne out by events. European collaboration was running into trouble on the political side when the grand design for a European army foundered on French suspicions, and Europe seemed on the point of retreating back into mutual suspicions and recriminations.

A compromise on the political question, the creation of the Western European Union which associated Britain with the Six at least in a limited sense, and the recognition of Germany as an equal member of N.A.T.O. saved the political situation. On the economic side, while the French were faltering, the torch was picked up by the European technocrats whom the new supranational and international bodies were bringing to the fore, and by the smaller nations who saw in European integration their own salvation.

The Six were to meet at Messina in 1955 to plan further cooperation. The political advance had been halted. It was to the economic question that the Six were to turn – to the vast and, it seemed, intractable problem of achieving a Common Market in all commodities, not merely in coal and steel.

At Messina it was agreed to set up a working party to evolve the details of such a move. With this working party and with the subsequent negotiations for a Common Market Treaty Britain was invited to join. After some initial gestures suggesting that it would take part, the British Government withdrew, announcing that it could not commit itself in advance, and that it would review the situation when agreement was reached.

This was to prove a fatal error. The British Government advisers, even at this stage, did not appear to have rated the chances of successful agreement very highly. They had the experience of France, with a relatively backward economy protected by high tariffs, to confirm their beliefs. To suppose that the French would accept a situation where they had to make prodigious steps towards efficiency or accept ruin in the face of German competition seemed unrealistic. As it happened, here too the British Government guessed wrong.

After eighteen months of bargaining and horse-trading the Six forged one of the decisive documents of twentieth-century history, the Treaty of Rome, the framework of a European Economic Community, and a blueprint for the Europe which was to achieve the unity that had foundered with the Roman Empire.

The Treaty of Rome

The Treaty laid down in broad detail the concept of the Common Market, or European Economic Community, to give it its official title.

The Common Market was to be created in stages, extending from 1958 to 1970 or 1973. The timetable envisaged the gradual reduction of tariffs between countries of the Community, and the progressive abolition of quotas and restrictions. It was planned that these tariff reductions would be of broadly ten per cent, at intervals normally of some eighteen months. There were to be three stages to the timetable, and the intention was to use the end of each stage as a breathing space if any country found that its economy was undergoing serious strain as a result of the fairly rapid pace. On the assumption that the delays which were permitted would not be invoked, it was anticipated that there would be free trade in all major industrial commodities by 1970. If the delays between stages had to be invoked it would take until 1973 to complete the process.

The progressive dismantling of tariffs between the member nations would be accompanied by the equalization of an external tariff, based on the average of the tariffs of the members. Thus, when complete, the Common Market could be a customs union with virtually free internal trade, and a common external tariff.

The main exception was to be agriculture, and it is in this field that the Market has been slowest to develop: here free trade was likely to prove a more complex business.

But plans for the Common Market went far further than a customs union. Within the Market there would be freedom of capital movement: if a German firm chose to build a new factory in, say, France, it would find no obstacles in its way, either from the German or the French Governments. For all practical purposes too there would be free movement of labour, and national frontiers would have little economic significance.

There were elaborate rules of competition and discrimination. Perhaps the most consequential was that, in order to put industry on an equal footing, social services in every country were to be brought to the same level. This in practice meant that the most generous provision in social security in any country would become obligatory in all the others, and so competition between a welfare-state industry and a low-cost industry with few social-security obligations would be avoided.

The financial and economic implications of the Treaty were enormous. The rights of each nation to direct its own economy would be so severely restricted that it would become scarcely realistic to regard the member nations as being independent national states. The original French dream of a supranational High Authority overseeing German heavy industry now seemed to foreshadow the realities of a unified Western Europe, for, with economic interdependence a reality, political independence would be a chimera.

The Treaty tackled the political realities boldly. It recognized that the political implications of a unified Europe were at least as important, and certainly as desirable, as the undoubted economic benefits.

114

It was a heady dream of a United Europe, and it was becoming a practical reality.

The Rome Treaty was the result of hard bargaining – bargaining from which Britain had quite deliberately excluded herself. Britain's credit had now been exhausted.

But even at this stage it was, or it appeared to be, open to Britain to join – but no longer to bargain – like any other European nation which was willing to subscribe to the principles of the Treaty.

It has sometimes been said by political cynics that if at this stage Britain had agreed unconditionally to join, then either the Treaty would have proved impractical or at least it would have had to be extensively renegotiated, for it was an elaborate compromise of national interests, which could scarcely have been left unaltered if a new member the size of Britain had applied to join.

What the British attempted to do was to bargain – two years too late. As it happened, however, their position appeared fairly strong, for the British arguments seemed to be supported by several valid points.

The first of the arguments was political. The Russian Government had scarcely been enthusiastic over the course of Western European integration. But the Common Market roused their vituperative powers to a new pitch. Its attractions for the countries of Eastern Europe and its drive towards European unity represented a threat to the Soviet position in Eastern Europe, and created an economic and political entity strongly anti-Communist in concept and rivalling in power either of the two super-powers. This was excellent for its members, firmly committed as they were to N.A.T.O. But the neutrals, who had braved Soviet anger by membership of the O.E.E.C., could join the Common Market only at the sacrifice of their jealously preserved neutrality.

The question which arose then was whether it was better to split Europe yet further by pressing the political implications of the Common Market, or whether it might not be better to concentrate on more economic cooperation, which could embrace a Free Trade Area comprising all of Western Europe, and not merely six N.A.T.O. members.

Any British initiative to create a non-political system would clearly have the backing of Europe's neutrals. Unfortunately, however, this was a policy which would scarcely commend itself to the six Common Market members: but, just as important, this was intensely unacceptable to the United States, which had enthusiastically endorsed the European movement as a significant step towards a strong Europe which could contain the Soviet threat.

The Free Trade Area suggested by Britain had attractions not only for the neutrals but also for the smaller European nations not yet involved with the Common Market. These nations, among them Norway and Denmark, had no desire to choose sides in a quarrel between Britain and the Six. Almost any compromise which would enable them to avoid siding with one or the other would have been acceptable, for with the prospects of rival tariff walls going up in Europe it would be exceedingly uncomfortable for these nations to make the choice.

The British plan was therefore designed to meet the problems of the neutrals and the smaller nations outside the Six. It proposed a European Free Trade Area, without political implications and equally accessible to all members of O.E.E.C., whether N.A.T.O. members or neutrals. It would operate on the same timetable as the Common Market, namely complete free trade in industrial goods by 1970. Agriculture was to be excluded.

Apart from its careful avoidance of political implications, the Free Trade plan also differed from the Treaty of Rome in two basic respects. It did not, firstly, require the elaborate system of free movements of capital and labour and equal social-security benefits; indeed it did not require the elaborate supranational system of the Common Market, with its implications of diminished national sovereignty which the British Government had so resolutely opposed.

Secondly, and this was to be a key factor, it did not envisage a common external tariff, as the Common Market did. Each nation would be allowed to retain its own tariffs, which would apply to non-members of E.F.T.A. This, claimed Britain, was essential if British membership was not to involve, not only the end of

Imperial Preference, but even perhaps a system whereby Britain might have to discriminate against Commonwealth imports.

Before the arguments are analysed in detail it must be said that the British Government found it hard even to get its ideas taken seriously. There was a strong suspicion, based on bitter experience in the 1950s, that the proposals were intended to put a spoke in the wheels of the Rome Treaty rather than to provide a reasonable substitute. It was only with much difficulty that the British were able to overcome the initial scepticism, and to get serious discussions going. The fact that the proposals were in the end taken seriously gives a tantalizing glimpse of what might have been, if the British had been as positive in their approach two or three years earlier.

The opposition to the British was now headed by the French. After their experience of the British, they were exceedingly sceptical about their somewhat tardy conversion to the ideal of European economic cooperation and were determined to ensure that the British plan should not under any circumstances lead to a postponement of the Rome Treaty timetable.

A procedural struggle ensued. The British wanted to place more importance on the international body which had served Western Europe so well in the 1950s, the O.E.E.C. The French wished negotiations to be conducted via the new supranational authorities which were overshadowing O.E.E.C. The French won – a decisive victory in its way, for it showed that the Six were explicitly committed to the supranational approach, with all its implications, distasteful both to the British and to the neutrals.

The French tactics were to delay negotiations as long as possible, and certainly until the end of 1958. For while the Common Market had been inaugurated at the beginning of 1958, the first ten per cent tariff cut was to take effect from 1 January 1959. Once the cut had been made, there was no turning back. The Common Market countries were committed. It would of course still be possible for Britain to apply for membership of the Common Market; but to alter it to the wider Free Trade Area would be unrealistic. In consequence the French pursued a course of extreme scepticism and minute examination of the British proposals.

So far as the British arguments were concerned, the purely political – or rather non-political – approach was not likely to raise much enthusiasm, especially so far as Germany, in all other aspects an advocate of British membership of a European system, was concerned. Certainly, too, Britain's reluctance to sacrifice a degree of national sovereignty, reflecting as it did an uncertainty of British aim and an unfortunate expression of remoteness, was not likely to endear her approach to those nations who in the first flush of enthusiasm saw in the Common Market a way out of the dead end of nationalism and the bloody wars which had caused so much misery in the continent, and dethroned it from world leadership.

The British attitude to the question of external tariffs was crucial. But what exactly were Britain's motives? On the face of it the argument was simply about Imperial Preference. If there were to be a common tariff, based on an average of members' tariffs, then Britain might well find not only that Imperial Preference was impossible, but even that she was compelled to impose a tariff where none had existed before against a Commonwealth member. The preferential tariff might be not only abolished, which would have been bad enough, but even reversed against its former beneficiaries. Although Common Market members had considerably less interest in the Commonwealth they might have recognized a legitimate British concern, for after all, they had already made accommodation for the French and other powers who had overseas dependencies.

Unfortunately there was another aspect of the whole problem, and this was the interest shown by outside powers and in particular the United States. The Common Market was potentially as rich a market as the U.S. home market, and it would grow at a faster rate. To compete effectively in this huge market American firms would require to invest substantially, to build new factories within the tariff walls, in one or other of the Common Market countries.

Where would American and other investment go? Already more than half the American investment in Europe was directed towards Britain. If this process were to be accelerated by British membership, on British terms, of a Free Trade Area, then American investment elsewhere would scarcely increase. The attraction of investment in Britain was that not only would this imply free access to all of Western Europe, but as a bonus, thanks to the Imperial Preference system and the Sterling Area arrangements, there would be a reasonable chance of preferential treatment there also. These advantages would be available nowhere else in Europe.

This would of course only be possible if the British proposals on differing national external tariffs were accepted. The Common Market countries could be excused some cynicism if they felt that this consideration as much as the Commonwealth attachment weighed heavily with the British negotiators.

Quite apart from the scepticism which the British attitude created, there were substantial arguments against the system of differing tariffs. If it was accepted, all that would happen, it was argued, was that in practice goods would be imported through whichever country had the lowest tariff and re-exported freely to any other country in the Free Trade Area. The British asserted that this problem could be avoided by the system of Certificates of Origin used in the Imperial Preference system. Suspect goods must be accompanied by such a certificate and any extra duty could be charged when goods moved within the Area. Unfortunately this would mean that a customs inspection would have to be made as goods passed from country to country within the Free Trade Area, whereas in the Common Market System customs posts would be abolished. Quite apart from the elaborate machinery of inspection there would be a problem of goods of mixed origin (i.e. processed partly outside the Area and partly inside). To each objection there was a solution, but the sum total of the solutions might be a complicated customs structure which was at variance with the ideal of a unified Europe. In spite of all attempts to simplify the procedure, little was achieved,

There was considerable willingness, even after years of British obstructiveness, among five of the nations at least to seek a European solution which would embrace Britain. But the French were adamant. They were convinced by experience that British membership would end hopes of European integration. In the last analysis, the other five nations had to choose between France, the good European, and Britain, whose past record was anything but good: inevitably when the crunch came they supported France.

The French delegation had only to keep the negotiations from succeeding until the first tariff cut – then it would be virtually impossible to substitute another scheme for the Common Market; and this they did.

Frustrated and angry the British delegation returned home, leaving the victory to France.

The Free Trade Association

If the negotiations had proved a fiasco for Britain, they were likely to prove even more of a disaster for some of the smaller nations. These now faced the problem of negotiating either with Britain or with the Common Market countries.

The next initiative came from one of these small countries – Sweden. Her proposals were in essence the British proposals for a Free Trade Area, cast in terms which were likely to attract the smaller nations.

To cut a complex story short, seven nations signed the Stockholm Convention in May 1959. They were a motley group, and it is worth considering their motives – for their mixture of motives was an indication of difficulties to come. In addition to Britain, there were three N.A.T.O. members, and three neutrals.

The three N.A.T.O. members, Norway, Denmark and Portugal, made their decision largely on the basis of economic self-interest. British trade was, on balance, more important than trade with the Six. The decision was of course far from easy. Either to join the Free Trade Area or to join the Common Market meant sacrifice in some market.

The three neutrals, Sweden, Switzerland and Austria, joined very much as a second best. The Russians, while disliking both groups, regarded the Free Trade Area with dislike but the Common Market with implacable hostility. On economic grounds the

Swedish case was perhaps marginal, but in the case of Switzerland and Austria, the natural economic grouping would have been with the Common Market, if economics, not politics, had been decisive.

The truth was that the Free Trade Association, sometimes called the Seven, or perhaps more significantly the Outer Seven, made little sense economically or politically. Scattered round the periphery of the Common Market, with diverse economic and social backgrounds, with political institutions varying from dictatorship to democracy, the nations were possibly as disparate a group as the continent could yield.

The difficulty of the Free Trade Association was that no one was entirely clear as to what its aim was. The Convention stated that one intention was to seek cooperation with the Common Market countries. In one sense the Free Trade grouping represented an attempt to achieve unity of purpose and aims, especially in negotiating with the Common Market countries. The theory was that better terms were more likely to be obtained collectively than individually.

Unfortunately this aim was not entirely compatible with the official concept of an economic union credible on its own account. As the negotiators were drawing up an official timetable for closer economic integration, they were simultaneously looking over their shoulders to plumb the reactions of the Common Market.

The Free Trade Association was conceived in uncertainty; and when it was born it proved a somewhat sickly infant with a most uncertain life expectation. Its timetable of tariff reductions was designed to coincide with that of the Common Market, so as to make the ultimate integration of the two that much easier when, or if, integration became possible. Since the Free Trade Area had been set up after the first ten per cent cut in the Common Market Tariffs, and because of the vastly different interests of the seven member nations, this was likely to prove exceedingly difficult. The difficult task was made almost impossible by the attitude of the Common Market to the new organization, for this was unmistakably hostile.

The Six did not regard the Seven as being at all complementary. Indeed they regarded E.F.T.A.'s existence as a positive obstacle to agreement. While they were willing to treat with individual nations, they were not interested in discussions with the Seven as a group. This hostility was shared by the United States, which, engaged in promoting the unity of an anti-Communist Europe, was very much inclined to regard the Seven as an obstacle to this aim. Indeed this attitude hardened when signs developed of a lessening of the Russian hostility towards the Free Trade Area, a development which could scarcely be for any other reason than that the Common Market–Free Trade split was well worth fostering.

No sooner had the Free Trade Association reached agreement, with many qualifications, on following the Common Market timetable than this was dramatically speeded up. It had originally been envisaged that tariffs would be reduced at eighteen-month intervals, so that the first stage would be complete by January 1962 with thirty per cent tariff cut.

Now it became clear that the Common Market countries were prepared to accelerate the timetable, not only in respect of internal tariff cuts but also in the adjustment towards the common external tariff. Since this was to be based on an average of the individual external tariffs it would clearly mean that a raising of the relatively low German tariff would be in part compensated by a lowering of the comparatively high French one. But the implications of an inevitable realignment of trade were ominous. The fact that for the time the Six were willing to follow an outward-looking policy and lower tariffs in accordance with international agreements was no guarantee that the economic split in Western Europe would not grow greater as time passed.

Changing attitudes

We have seen that the French were largely the originators of the Common Market concept, with its emphasis on the supranational authorities, and a willingness to accept British participation. But time had passed, motives had changed. The original design of containing Germany had been replaced by the grander one of European unity. Perhaps indeed the goal of European unity reflected the dismal failure of the France of the Fourth Republic, which foundered in military revolt, and an upsurge of French patriotism, personified in de Gaulle.

Whatever one might say of General de Gaulle, and few British statesmen in the early 1960s had much to say in his favour, his impact on France and on Europe was dramatic. He has been presented as anti-British. So in a sense he was, but the picture was oversimplified, indeed caricatured, almost beyond recognition. General de Gaulle first and foremost believed in France, and then in a Europe powerful in its own right, and at least the equal of the two super-powers. By implication, he was prepared to see Europe and America parting their ways and his hostility to Britain was to her role, as he saw it, as the lesser of the Anglo-Saxon powers, and as the tool in Europe of the greater of the two.

But beneath the antipathy which he was to arouse in Britain, it is important to realize just how close his logic lay to that of the British. He was a nationalist and patriot, not one of the new breed of European technocrats who were in control of the Common Market, and whom he distrusted far more than the British did. French policy, like British policy, was being turned upside down. De Gaulle in 1960 was no more ready to sacrifice French sovereignty to a supranational authority than Attlee was in 1950. Indeed the ironic part of the subsequent negotiations has been that, as the British reluctantly moved towards that sacrifice of national sovereignty which would have gained them so much in the early days, the French were moving back to the concept of national independence which had been Britain's stumbling block in the past. The only difference was that the French were in the Common Market and the British were not.

To understand what was to happen in the next few years one must always bear in mind that it was not only the British who had changed their stance, but, at least as important, so had the French. Moreover it was clear that, although from now on British membership of the Common Market was to be supported by the expansionists, the internationalists and the technocrats of the

Headquarters at Brussels, and opposed by the proud nationalist leader of a recuperating France, the British Government, still hankering after a world role as well as a European one, had in the last analysis at least as much in common with its opponent as with its allies.

In the meantime, however, the two major blocs proceeded on their separate ways. The Common Market was proving an exceptional success. In only one field – agriculture – was it showing any sign of failure. For the rest it was going from strength to strength, and its rate of growth far exceeded that of Britain, the Free Trade Area or the United States.

E.F.T.A. was enjoying only moderate success. Trade was growing between member nations, but so too, at rather a faster rate, was trade between the Six and members of E.F.T.A. The second-best nature of the arrangement was beginning to make itself more obvious; E.F.T.A. was a market of about eighty or ninety million people, enjoying in general a high standard of living, but with a slower rate of growth than the Six. The Common Market home area had about 180 million people and was growing, and it was to the Common Market rather than to the Seven that the uncommitted nations were now looking. Indeed there was evidence that members of the Seven themselves were having second thoughts on their choice.

To a very large extent the initiative within the Seven lay with Britain. Some members were waiting with ill-concealed impatience for a British initiative to break the deadlock with the Six. Only the neutrals had reservations about such a move. For the rest, countries such as Denmark and possibly Norway had much to gain from a British lead which would take them into the Common Market.

It was becoming clear that not only was the Free Trade Association relatively unsuccessful: it was potentially an obstacle to progress, as the Common Market countries had prophesied. For if, in the end, the members of the Seven had to negotiate individually with the Six, then the commitments which countries like Britain had made in the Stockholm Convention might very well prove stumbling blocks to the success of any negotiations. Not only would it be difficult to reach agreement that would satisfy the political aims of the Six and the neutrals of the Seven, but also there were strong grounds for saying that, even if the Six could become seven by including Britain without their aims becoming too diffuse, for all seven E.F.T.A. countries to join more or less simultaneously would end the feeling of European unity which had been the driving force of the Common Market.

Even such a petty point as linguistic precedence was likely to play its part. The French were fiercely proud of their language, the language of diplomacy, which, though retreating before the pervading influence of English elsewhere, could still be the lingua franca of the Common Market. The admission of the United Kingdom and Scandinavia would almost certainly encourage the wider use of English instead. Perhaps a trivial point, but in the context of growing French nationalism one not to be ignored.

The first twenty per cent tariff cut by the Free Trade Association coincided with the Common Market's second ten per cent cut in July 1960. But by January 1962, in spite of some friction on agricultural policy, the Common Market countries were not only prepared to move into the second stage, they were down to the sixty per cent level of the 1950 tariffs and accelerating progress. It was clear that the Common Market would be complete long before the planned date of 1970.

Fortunately, as we have seen, the Common Market countries were so far pursuing a very moderate policy over their external tariffs and, while these were being gradually standardized, there were few signs of a high tariff wall. Just the same, each tariff cut increased the dilemma of the countries outside, and a number of these began to make tentative inquiries about associate membership of the Market, a form designed primarily for members' ex-colonial territories and which did not carry the same political commitments as full membership. The position of the Free Trade countries was far from happy as they contrasted the rapidly growing integration of the Six with their own less spectacularly successful programme.

The situation was changed in 1961 by the volte-face of the British Government. Having spurned the Common Market in the past they now announced their intention of negotiating for membership. The news was greeted with relief by the N.A.T.O. members of the Seven, with mixed feelings by the neutrals, according to their vulnerability to Soviet pressure, with pleasure among most of the Common Market countries, and with considerable reserve by the French.

The negotiations of 1962

The decision to seek membership of the Common Market was made by the Prime Minister, Harold Macmillan, in July 1961. He stated at the time that British membership would depend on the effects on the Commonwealth, the Free Trade Area, and British agriculture.

It was decided on behalf of the Common Market countries that as far as possible they would present a joint point of view and that the Commission of the Community should take part in the conference as adviser to the Six.

Membership of the Six would also involve membership of the Coal and Steel Community and of Euratom, the European Atomic Energy Authority, which had been set up at the same time as the Common Market. This was accepted by the British Government, which also announced its unqualified acceptance of the aims of the Rome Treaty, including the elimination of internal tariffs, the common external tariff, and a common commercial and agricultural policy. Any changes in the Community in respect of transitional arrangements could be made by adding protocols to the Rome Treaty, not by altering it in substance.

The subsequent negotiations on tariff duties on a number of Commonwealth goods entering Britain were exceedingly complex and of technical interest only. The following points were established: that the British timetable on the common tariff would have to be modified; that sympathetic treatment might be considered for the underdeveloped countries, and also for New Zealand, which was so heavily dependent on the British market for butter.

The butter issue, as it turned out, was only a part of the very much larger problem of Common Market agricultural policy, which remained unresolved throughout the negotiations. At the risk of oversimplification it might be said that the British system of subsidies for her own farmers, cheap food imports from the Commonwealth and dearer imports from elsewhere would have to be replaced in a few years' time by a system geared to the Common Market: but that since the Common Market system was still very much a matter of dispute the British Government were reluctant to make extensive revisions which might then have to be revised within a very short time.

One of the most delicate problems of the whole negotiations was of course Britain's relationship with the Free Trade Association. While it would legally be possible on one year's notice to withdraw from E.F.T.A., the moral obligation to the other members could not lightly be repudiated, and in its preliminary announcement of its intention to negotiate the British Government had made it clear that it would require satisfactory arrangements to be made on the Free Trade Area question. Fortunately the British position was eased by the readiness with which members of E.F.T.A., with the exception of Finland (an associate member), applied either for membership, associate membership or some form of relationship with the Common Market. In the case of E.F.T.A. countries applying for full membership, the problem would obviously be made easier to resolve. The question of the neutrals who applied for less than full membership, and were obviously anxious to avoid political commitment, was a good deal less tractable.

During the negotiations occurred that fateful Commonwealth Conference at which the British Government found itself facing a barrage of criticism from other members. Imperial Preference, fading as it was, had a good deal of life left in it. The bitterest criticism came from the two extremes, the Canadian Conservative Government under Mr Diefenbaker, and the new members (of whom Ghana was typical), who were highly suspicious of the political implications of the Common Market. These extremes found themselves able to unite in their objections to the prospective loss of preferential treatment in British markets. But it became fairly clear that the Commonwealth governments were not particularly anxious to extend preferential treatment to British imports, or indeed to come up with an alternative to resolve Britain's difficulty as her traditional Commonwealth markets dwindled behind tariffs imposed by the Commonwealth governments. Ironically the greatest degree of understanding, if not entirely of sympathy, for the British problem came from the country which had most to lose, New Zealand.

The Conference was a climacteric. It established irrevocably the bona fides of the British Government in its determination to reach a settlement with the Six. It established too the fact that the Commonwealth link was no real substitute for the Common Market, for it was made abundantly clear that none of the Commonwealth countries, however anxious to retain a privileged position in the United Kingdom market, was prepared to offer very much in return. Finally, although it aroused considerable emotion at the time about the strength of Commonwealth feeling, the hostility and negative attitude towards British economic problems engendered a certain amount of disillusion about some of the lofty ideas of Commonwealth unity.

In the meantime negotiations dragged on apparently endlessly. The French delegation in particular insisted, as in the previous negotiations in 1958, upon a minute examination of the implications of all the concessions which the Six and the Commission were prepared to offer. Although these tactics apparently irritated the other five nations – the 'friendly five' as they were to become – the French delegation were able to keep the negotiations down to a snail's pace.

It appears likely that France's intention was to provoke the British delegation into breaking off negotiations, as had happened four years previously. But this time the British were to prove as obdurate as the French. Both made a serious error in calculation, the French in assuming that the British would lose patience before they did, and the British in assuming that if the other five nations were solidly on Britain's side on a particular issue, the French would give way. To the British delegation it appeared that, irritating as the delay was, opinion within the E.E.C. was hardening against French obstructionism.

When the break came, however, it had nothing to do with economic matters. President de Gaulle had little regard for the economic side at all. The fatal flaw in the British application so far as he was concerned was the so-called special relationship with the United States. The meeting between Macmillan and de Gaulle at Rambouillet was followed by the Nassau meeting with President Kennedy, in which the British Government made it only too clear, from France's point of view, that they were more concerned about relations with the U.S. than with France. To permit Britain to enter the Common Market would, in de Gaulle's view, be to admit a country which would be prepared to act on behalf of America in frustrating the French grand design for a Europe independent of both America and the Eastern Bloc.

To the consternation of the other five as well as of Britain, the President, at a dramatic Press Conference in Paris in January 1963, slammed the door on British entry, and yet another chapter closed in the unhappy story of Britain's relations with Europe.

It was easy, indeed it has proved all too easy, to blame de Gaulle and the French for what happened. But in the early stages of the move towards European integration it was the British who had ruined their own chances. It was a stroke of irony perhaps that in 1958 de Gaulle inherited a position in Europe which had been prepared for him by men for whose supranational aspirations he could have felt little but antipathy, and which he was able to exploit skilfully to further his own ideals. But if de Gaulle had done little to deserve the inheritance of European goodwill the British Government at that time had done even less.

Moreover, it would be unwise to assume that, even had the French not vetoed the British application when they did, all the negotiations would have reached a satisfactory conclusion. A very large number of problems was still outstanding; soluble problems admittedly, but by their very number likely to require considerable negotiation. The easy identification of the French as the villains of the piece could lead to yet another unpleasant shock when serious negotiations are resumed. The extent of the difficulties other than French intransigence which have yet to be solved may prove to be much greater than is commonly realized.

Passions have died down. The failure of the negotiations has not been the disaster prophesied, and the last chapter has not been written on the matter.

But if the effect of the French veto was considerable in Britain, it was equally traumatic in Europe.

The negotiations had at least established that whatever might have been Britain's attitude in the past, she was wholeheartedly committed to the principle of cooperation with Europe. The attitude of the French had been made equally clear and the good-will accumulated had been lost. The bargains which were to be struck from time to time after the failure would once again be between sovereign states in return for a *quid pro quo*. Much of the idealism had gone, to be replaced, at least in so far as relations with France were concerned, by a cold-blooded estimate of gain or loss.

The other European nations

The situation of the smaller European nations at the time when an economic and social split was developing between the Common Market and Free Trade Area was not easy. Their subsequent attitude was determined largely by the political facts of life, facts over which they had little control.

The Russians' attitude to the Free Trade Area modified significantly, however. No doubt they had begun to appreciate the possibilities inherent in a split in Western Europe and felt it was to their interests to bolster the weaker of the two groups, the Free Trade Association. In any event Russian hostility to Finland's membership diminished; in return for trade concessions they withdrew their objections to an association between Finland and the Seven, and in July 1961 she became an associate member.

The other two outsiders in Northern Europe were Iceland and Ireland. Iceland's interest in free trade in industrial goods was perhaps minimal, although she had an obvious interest in the Norwegian attempts to have fish imports thus classified. The time of the negotiations coincided with a dispute on fishing rights with Britain, and this perhaps prevented her following the Scandinavian countries into the Free Trade Association. Her interests and importance in industrial free trade have been small.

Eire's economy, unpalatable as the fact may be to Irish politicians, is entirely dependent on the British market. During the 1962 negotiations between Britain and the Common Market, the Irish made it clear that they were interested in membership, even if the political consequences affected Irish neutrality – and indeed the Common Market principle might have led the way to a solution of the perennial partition dispute. But with the failure of Britain's negotiations, the question of Irish membership receded.

Moving round the periphery of Europe, we find that Spain was in an equally difficult position. The natural economic link for Spain was the Common Market. But the Spanish economy was in no condition to stand up to competition from the more efficient industry of France and Germany. Besides this the Spanish Government disliked the implications of economic and political liberalization inherent in the Common Market: these had weighed in Portugal's decision to opt for the Free Trade Area. The Spaniards have shown interest in associate membership, however, and with increasing liberalization of the régime and modernization of industry they may in time become full-fledged members. But any economic division between Spain and Portugal would merely emphasize the unhappy consequences of the split which now exists in Europe – if indeed the Portuguese did not in turn also join the Common Market.

The position of Greece and Turkey was distinctly peripheral, both geographically and economically. Neither economy could stand up to unrestricted competition from the industrial nations of either bloc. Their relations with Britain were strained, at the time of the negotiations, over the problem of Cyprus. At the moment Greece and Turkey are associate members of the Common Market.

It is fairly clear that all nations outside the Iron Curtain will in the end adhere to one bloc or the other. If at the end there is a measure of agreement between the two blocs European unity will become very much a practical proposition. But if the split continues it is likely to involve all Europe.

Changing attitudes – the United Kingdom and the United States

Attitudes, political and economic, tend to change with a deflating rapidity. What seems a self-evident proposition, a fact of life which is virtually immutable, in one decade may be quite drastically revised in the next. The dollar gap which seemed so formidable and permanent in the late 1940s had ten years later become history, and the dollar itself had changed from one of the most desirable currencies into one which was under some suspicion.

The latest of such dramatic changes in attitude probably relates to the Common Market. The official British attitude has veered from scepticism to an almost blind faith in membership as a panacea for British economic ills: in its last months the Tory Government appeared to be veering back to scepticism, under the impact of the visible deterioration in relations between member countries, and the substitution of hard bargaining between nation states for the idealism of the middle 1950s.

The original scepticism had, of course, been based on the conviction that the nations of Western Europe, traditionally hostile to one another and jealous of their natural sovereignty, would be unable to sink their differences. In particular this was a political scepticism, but it was matched on the economic side by the improbability that the French economy, traditionally backward compared with German industry, and heavily protected, could modernize itself so rapidly as to be able to compete effectively once the barriers came down. The political and economic acumen of France was badly underestimated in Britain at this time.

The success, against all the probabilities, of the Common Market, and the very rapid growth rate of the economies of the Common Market countries contrasted markedly with the state of affairs in Britain, where the boom years for the Common Market were a period of stop-go economic stagnation, or at best of slow growth. There was perhaps a tendency to assume that British membership would automatically confer this characteristic rapid growth, without much consideration of the root causes of Britain's failure to expand at anything like the same rate. It is possible of course that the psychological shock of entry might have had a rejuvenating effect on the British economy and created conditions of rapid growth. But this was by no means a foregone conclusion.

Over-enthusiastic exponents of joining tended to draw horrific pictures of Britain sinking, if she failed to join, to the status of impoverished offshore islands. The disastrous effects of British failure to join have not entirely materialized, and this, combined with the deterioration of relations between members of the Six and a slowing down of the rate of growth, has possibly led to an excessive reaction against future membership. But it is not always appreciated that, even after the recent deterioration, the Common Market is growing at a rate which the British economy would find it hard to match. Moreover, while the immediate effects of Britain's exclusion have not been disastrous, the long-term advantages which will accrue for members of the Six are still as potent as ever. However shaky the political foundations of the Common Market seem, its economic foundations are as strong as ever. Yet more ominous from Britain's point of view is the fact that the failure to gain admittance to the Six left her without any obvious alternative, since E.F.T.A. was too small, and the Commonwealth countries were not very willing to accept increased British exports.

If the British attitude to the Common Market has been changeable, the reaction in America from enthusiasm to something approaching disillusion has been almost as marked. The American Government since the end of the Second World War had favoured European cooperation. Distance perhaps, and a certain oversimplification of the situation, had led them to believe that in a federal Europe would be found all the merits Americans discerned in their own system of government. When federation, as a practical proposition, seemed to recede, they lent all their support to any movement which would unify Europe economically. Their insistence, during Marshall Aid negotiations, on dealing with an international organization representing Europe rather than with individual countries illustrated this approach.

They watched with growing approval the emergence of the

supranational authorities, and actively encouraged the creation of a Common Market. Britain was the particular target for American pressure to join, and her tendency to hold aloof evoked considerable criticism.

Their attitude towards the European Free Trade Association was one of disapproval. To the Americans the Common Market was the economic counterpart to N.A.T.O.; and any organization which, like E.F.T.A., included neutrals was regarded as a mere instrument likely to split Europe and weaken the anti-Soviet front. When in 1961 the British Government reversed its policy and applied for membership of the Six, the support it received from the United States was considerable – so much so that it gave some substance to the French claim that the British were to enter as America's go-between.

The Americans were acutely aware that the Europe of the Common Market would have to organize its production on American lines for American-style mass-production for a mass market. It is at least possible that they were more complacent about the implied flattery of imitation than they were worried by the implications of rivalry.

That the Common Market will prove a formidable rival to American industry is certain, and the massive investment by American industrialists showed that the private sector of the American economy was aware of this. The history of the Six has shown that their relations with the United States are likely to be far from smooth. There are perhaps two reasons for this. The rise to power within the Community of General de Gaulle, who was particularly concerned to demonstrate his independence from the United States, was matched by a wave of European self-assertiveness and an unwillingness to treat America as anything other than a trade rival. In the protection of European interests, instanced perhaps by the slightly ridiculous but highly significant 'chicken war' designed to exclude American frozen chickens from the German market, the Common Market has shown itself to be uninhibited in its approach to its erstwhile mentor and benefactor. This obduracy has been repeated in the tariff negotiations of 1964–7 conducted under the aegis of the

General Agreement on Tariffs and Trade. While it would be stretching the point to claim that America created the Common Market, the Americans may yet feel, when they contemplate the inroads that the Six are likely to make into traditional American markets, that they have helped to create a Frankenstein monster.

Britain and Europe in the 1960s

The 1960s proved, in fact, to be a transition period – for Britain awaiting a change in the attitude of France, which clearly had the power to veto her entry into the Common Market, and for the Common Market itself as the French veto destroyed the idealism of the late 1950s and replaced it with a European Economic Community which was unlikely to move very fast towards its ideal of European unity.

For a time after the failure of the 1962 negotiations British trade with the Six increased fast. This was partly due to the intense interest in the European market which the ill-fated negotiations had stimulated; partly it was due to the initially outward-looking tariff policy of the Six.

British exports to Germany had been high throughout the post-war period. Now, as the common tariff took shape, the markets of Italy and France, previously very heavily protected, began to open up for British exporters at the very time when both these countries were experiencing a significant rise in national income.

The satisfactory rise in British exports to the Common Market countries may however prove a somewhat transient phenomenon since it depends on combining the advantages of falling external tariff rates, with the continued if temporary existence of internal tariffs. Recent experience suggests that the rise in British exports to the Six is now slowing down.

The advantages for British exporters may to some extent be continued if tariff reductions under the General Agreement on Tariffs and Trade can continue to lower trade barriers as in the past, but the success or failure of this is something in which the British Government will have little to say. The real negotiations will take place between the Common Market countries and the United States – and the auspices are not very favourable.

As a precaution against the widening gap between Britain and the Common Market, British industrialists have, over the past few years, built up subsidiary factories within the Common Market – though this method of trade is not likely to prove a complete alternative to membership.

In spite of the increase in British exports to the Six, it must be remembered that the Common Market economies have been expanding at a faster rate than the British. As a basis for expanding exports, the acceptance of a lower rate of economic growth can hardly be regarded as satisfactory.

Almost, one suspects, as an afterthought, determined efforts were made by the British Government to give more reality to the economic side of E.F.T.A., and this was indeed successful to some extent. But the whole future of E.F.T.A. has been thrown into jeopardy by the public admission of its inadequacies, and it would be optimistic to assume that its future is secure. A period of intense reappraisal of both blocs was inevitable, firstly because of the British application for Community membership, and even more so since it failed.

The situation within the Common Market was puzzling. The great disappointment of the 'friendly five' at the French veto brought a good deal of latent resentment against France to the surface. Yet the supporters of the British case found themselves in a cruel dilemma. They disapproved of what de Gaulle had done, but they could scarcely carry their disapproval to the point of wrecking the Community. Willy-nilly they had to a large extent to accept the French line as the maximum possible advance for the European Community. They were not helped by the fact that the British Labour party, who, if the public opinion polls were to be believed, were likely to form the next Government, had taken a strongly anti-European line during the negotiations. Was it worth holding up Europe's advance to unity for a nation which might spurn their aims?

In an international crisis it is rare for one side to be entirely in the right, and the subsequent action of some of the friendly five was perhaps as dubiously justified by the spirit of the Rome Treaty as the de Gaulle veto had been. The greatest clash came once again on agriculture. The German Government's unwillingness to sacrifice the interests of its farming community to the increased efficiency of French agriculture had almost caused a crisis in the period 1961–2 when the Common Market was about to move on to the second of its three stages. Then the Germans had made concessions to the French viewpoint. The situation repeated itself in 1964 when the German Government, conscious that the agriculture vote was crucial to its own prospects of staying in office at the 1965 elections, dug its heels in against French demands for the implementation of a European plan for agricultural marketing. Even the smaller nations of the Six, which had been so opposed to France's attitude over Britain, could not but support the French point of view. Yet it is a little doubtful whether the obvious and perhaps justified exasperation of the French over the continued protection of a relatively inefficient sector of the German economy gained as much sympathy among the other nations as it might have done had the French not sacrificed so much good will.

In the long run, the French were fairly certain to win, although they had to indulge in some fairly explicit threats of breaking away from the Common Market to achieve their goal. The Germans finally gave way and largely accepted French policy on agricultural prices. However shaken the political idealism of the European movement might have been, the economic problems were being solved.

Even though stresses were showing in the internal structure of the Common Market, its power and influence in the world scene was growing. It was an ironic commentary on the hostility displayed by members of the Commonwealth towards the British application for membership that, in little over a year after its failure, several of the Commonwealth countries who had been most critical were making their individual approaches to the Six. Nigeria, Kenya, Uganda and Tanganyika led the applicants but there was little doubt that others would follow.

The renewed attempts by the Labour Government in 1966 and

1967 to win membership had as little success as the Conservative attempts of previous years, though there was no spectacular climax on this occasion. The fact that the Common Market survived what was in effect yet another French veto was a tribute to its economic strength. But the fact too that now both the major political parties in the United Kingdom had committed themselves to the ideal of ultimate membership meant that the new Conservative Government could possibly win approval from both major parties if negotiations, renewed in 1970, bore fruit: and de Gaulle's retirement in France gave some hope of success.

The case for the Common Market

The economic case for the Common Market or a similar bloc can be summed up in one word – size.

It is a characteristic of many industries today that, with the appearance of new methods of production, firms become larger and fewer. Designs become more complex, and the time-span between the designing of a component and its finally coming off the assembly line may be years. Immense expense is incurred without return for these years of planning, and if the product is finally to make a profit it will do so only after a year or two of production on a massive scale.

A good example of this is the British car industry. Initially there was a great number of small firms producing individual models – perhaps a few hundred of each model, at a selling price far beyond the reach of the man in the street. The period from design to production was not long; indeed cars could be built to the specifications of any individual who was prepared to pay.

Today there are very few car firms producing popular cars in Britain. But the cars produced are standardized, except for superficial differences of colour and accessories, they are cheap, and they are produced by the hundred thousand. Mass-production and standardization permit an immense lowering of unit-cost, and these of course are practical only in a mass market.

Britain, with over fifty million inhabitants and enjoying a high standard of living, is large enough to support such a mass-production industry. But a country like the United States with a population nearly four times as large and a higher standard of living is even more advantageously placed. Relatively a car is a much cheaper item in the U.S.A. than in Britain, and the scale of production is a large factor in this.

There are some manufactured items which can apparently be mass-produced in the U.K. with all the advantages of a large market: radios, television sets, refrigerators, and so on. There is a number of manufactures, however, whose technical feasibility is less certain, given the size of the market. The aircraft industry, for example, is at a considerable disadvantage compared with the United States, and this disadvantage is likely to grow, as aircraft become larger and more complicated and the number which must be sold before a particular design 'breaks even' grows. Although of course many of the sales take place overseas, a large home market which will be prejudiced in favour of the home product is an excellent base from which to sell aircraft internationally.

Essentially, then, this is the economic case for the Common Market. Countries of Western Europe with a home market of about fifty million at the most will find their market increased to about 180 million and, with membership increased to include Britain and the other applicants, it might well exceed 250 million. A home market of this size, with a high standard of living, is comparable to that of the United States – and in view of the relative rates of growth of America and the Common Market, it is conceivable that by the end of the century this could be the larger market.

How will this affect European industry? Almost certainly it will accelerate the move towards an American scale of production, and American methods. It is possible, for example, to foresee in an industry like car production that Europe might be dominated by three or four huge firms planning production not by the hundred thousand, but by the million.

Naturally the attitude of a particular industry towards European integration depends very much on whether or not it has reason to fear increased competition in its home markets; and on

139

whether it can increase its share of a Common Market or fears to lose its hold in a national market. Some industries have clear technological reasons to be confident, others to be anxious. For many, the imponderables are too great and the reactions of their managers and workers tend to be emotional – the Common Market is felt to be an opportunity or else a menace.

Already inside Europe the amalgamation process is going on, on an international scale. Indeed one criticism levelled at the Common Market is that its attitude towards monopoly and cartels is less severe than it might be.

In general terms, the position of British industry is strong, but any potential advantage is growing less. British industry, in spite of the numerous criticisms levelled against it, is technically advanced in most sectors, and is certainly comparable to any in Europe. The British home market has been larger than that of any individual Common Market country, since her population equals the largest in Western Europe, and enjoys a standard of living which was until recently higher than any of the Six. The British market was therefore the largest and wealthiest single market; so, other things being equal, British industry had a slight edge over possible rivals.

But the advantage has lessened and is still lessening. As the tariffs are going down in Europe national markets are being trebled or quadrupled and European industry is accommodating itself to this increase. Simultaneously the rapid growth of national income in the Common Market is matched by a rise in living standards to the British level if not beyond it. Clearly time is not on the side of British industry.

If the economics of marketing lie so heavily in favour of the Common Market, why then are some British economists opposed to British entry? Apart perhaps for some special pleading on behalf of particular industries and some reserve felt on the possible effects on British food prices, the main arguments against joining are in a sense negative. They in fact dispute that a market of over 200 million people has a very much greater value than one of over fifty million. The advantages of increased size are theoretically unanswerable, but the technical difficulties which might arise in such a large and complex market would outweigh them. Mass-production for a market of fifty million has all the practical advantages of a market several times that size, so these opponents of British membership would claim. If this were true then the economic case for joining would be unproved and a decision against the Market could be made on political grounds.

It is not intended here to argue the merits or demerits on the economic side in any greater detail. The point of the argument that the economic case is not proven merely re-emphasizes the fact that the Common Market is basically a political as well as an economic organization. The economic arguments by themselves are but one aspect of the problem and anyone who attempts to assess the matter on purely economic grounds, without having any political opinions, is analysing the problem in unrealistic terms.

Monetary problems of the European Economic Community

If the European Economic Community is to be more than a rather extensive customs union, national autonomy within the Community is likely to be further reduced. One of the more important of the fields where it has already been reduced is that of independent monetary and financial policies. Logically, as the Community grows closer and closer, the use of trade restrictions or quotas to deal with an individual country's balance of payments problems with the rest of the Community will be more and more circumscribed.

What steps would be available, then, to any country which suffered from a persistent balance of payments problem? It might in theory alter its exchange rate (i.e. devalue), although the practical results of such a policy would be very great and would affect the confidence on which the free capital movements throughout the Community depend. In practice the political effects on the Community of such a step would be so great as to make it a very remote possibility indeed. Alternatively, it might be possible to alter internal monetary policy, raising interest rates and, if necessary, carrying out deflationary measures. Finally, a country in difficulty might be able to rely on its foreign-currency reserves, bearing in mind that capital might well be moved in from other parts of the Community.

Once the Rome Treaty timetable has been completed the situation of the Community's balance of payments would be in some respects analogous to any situation which could arise within a single country; and the same sort of mechanism which prevents a balance-of-payments crisis arising between, for example, England and Scotland, or California and New York, would operate. The imbalance of payments would in the long run mean that ownership of more and more assets in that particular country would pass into the hands of nationals of other member states of the Community, and this will in a sense have little more significance than a change in the distribution of national income within a single country – indeed it might well be much less significant. That nationals of one country of the Community should have large investments in another is regarded as a natural feature of such a Community, and the free movement of capital merely accelerates the process.

In practice the natural forces of the market would tend to limit changes. One country which was constantly experiencing the sort of economic difficulties which might have given rise to currency problems would probably find either that more industry moved in, or conceivably that labour, which generally remits cash homewards, would move to some other region, even across frontiers.

Ultimately of course one would expect complete economic integration to be followed by monetary integration. The eventual establishment of a common European currency is a logical consequence of successful economic integration in other respects.

Clearly, however, a common currency is still a long way off and there is a number of very great hurdles, not least of which would be its irreversibility, the scrambling of the eggs, so to speak. An intermediate step might be an attempt to set up national currencies in units which were at a par one with another (i.e. one

French franc = one Deutschmark, etc.). A certain amount of foreign-note circulation might then be acceptable without too much difficulty, just as in practice pound notes issued by Scottish Banks can be used without much difficulty in England. The importance of the note issue of any central bank is of course small compared with the 'Bank Money', cheques, bills of exchange, etc., which are the really important forms of currency circulation in a modern society. The mutual acceptance of foreign banknotes might seem of little import, but psychologically it would have a tremendous impact in the creation of a European nationalism.

In time of course such a mutual acceptance could lead gradually not to the creation of a Central Bank for Europe so much as a Federal Reserve system such as operates in the United States, where twelve Federal Reserve Banks fulfil the functions of the single central bank of most countries. Certainly there seems to be plenty of scope for even closer cooperation between the central banks than now exists.

How long this ideal of a unified banking system and a European currency will take to emerge is problematic. That it is the logical outcome not only of the European movement since the end of the war, but also of the closer cooperation of all central banks in averting crises is clear.

Any decisions on these matters may be vitally important to the future of the United Kingdom. It is therefore the more unfortunate that Britain's influence on the decisions will be at best marginal.

Chapter 5

INTERNATIONAL EQUILIBRIUM

IN Chapter 2 the inadequacies of present arrangements to provide for an international currency were discussed briefly. It is in theory possible to do without an international currency, just as it is to do without an internal currency, if one is prepared to accept barter rather than trade as a method of exchanging goods. The practical inconveniences of barter are enormous, depending as it does on a mutual coincidence of wants: not only must you have something to exchange that is wanted by someone else, but he must have, to exchange for it, exactly what you want.

One of the great merits, and one of the prime functions, of money is as a store of value. It is a commodity which can be acquired by trade, and kept in reserve to be used on another occasion. If we apply this principle to international trade we can see the enormous advantage of each nation having a reserve 'store of value', that is, a reserve of an international currency. Armed with such a reserve a nation need not balance day by day, or even year by year, its sales and purchases, or indeed its lending and borrowing, with the rest of the world, but can trade with a fair degree of freedom, occasionally adding to its reserves of international currency, occasionally dipping into them. If, however, a nation is suffering from a shortage of these reserves, this ready cash, so to speak, it may be forced to restrict its trading, to erect barriers to the free exchange of goods, not because of any fundamental problem but because of a shortage of immediately available reserves.

When one nation runs short of these international reserves, the situation is unfortunate enough. When the world as a whole is short of them it is even more serious, rather as if, in a perfectly sound economy, the medium of exchange (i.e. money) had become so short that the economy was being forced back to a barter stage. The twin problems of international liquidity are to ensure that no one nation need be compelled by a temporary shortage of international reserves to resort to restriction and barter tactics, and that the world as a whole does not run short of these international reserves. The continued growth of relatively free international trade depends upon a satisfactory solution, and this chapter discusses some of the aspects of these problems – the concept of international equilibrium.

The precursors of the International Monetary Fund

A problem that has recurred constantly in the postwar years is international liquidity – or very crudely the amount of international monetary reserves which are required to keep the machinery of international trade well lubricated. It is unrealistic to expect each nation constantly and instantaneously to keep its accounts balanced with every other nation. A nation might in general terms be paying its way with the rest of the world, yet find seasonal fluctuations in its earning capacity or its needs for foreign exchange. A nation relying on the sale of a crop might find itself acquiring a vast surplus of foreign exchange in one month, and yet be in deficit for the other eleven months. Conversely a nation with a steady export income throughout the year might find that at one period, when buying a crop for example, it suffered a temporary embarrassment for funds.

Thus just as a business might need a certain quantity of ready cash or liquid assets, so a nation requires a supply of foreign exchange or gold to meet month-to-month variations. If a nation is seriously short of such ready cash it may be compelled to restrict trade to meet what is merely a temporary phase, and the whole pattern of trade and international development could be distorted thereby. What is in this context required, ideally, is some form of international currency acceptable to all, which nations could use to meet everyday transactions without having to resort to restrictions which are, in the long run, really unnecessary.

The ideal international currency would probably be gold: but there are two practical difficulties. There is not nearly enough gold in the world to supply all the international currency needed, and what there is is not equitably distributed. In practice national currencies, among them sterling, are used as a substitute. The difficulties of using national currencies as the basis of international liquidity are considerable and they are likely to increase. Thus as international trade grows, the amount of international currency, or liquidity, required increases, and the second-best nature of the present arrangements becomes increasingly obvious.

The problem of international liquidity is comparatively new, at least in its present form. During the pre-1914 period of the gold standard the difficulties were not immediately obvious. There was relatively a good deal more gold circulating freely. Obviously there was less gold available in absolute terms, but its price was high in terms of the prices then prevailing and there was no real shortage. The role of sterling was greater: there was no shortage of it, and its widespread use was not likely to cause Britain any inconvenience too great to be borne. But in the last resort the gold standard tended to keep the growth rate of an economy bounded by its commitments in the international field. There could be no real problem of international liquidity while the gold basis of the currency circulating was, in theory at least, available for export. That such gold exports did not occur extensively reflected the fact that an imbalance of trade such as would lead to a currency crisis, would be cured by a change in the level of employment. There was no liquidity crisis in this period for the simple reason that it would not have been allowed to develop.

So far as the United Kingdom was concerned the period of the 1920s was one of severe deflation aimed at raising the value of sterling. Again the problem could be contained by accepting a lower level of employment.

The 1930s ushered in the new era of the floating exchange rate. After 1931 sterling was left to find its own level in the foreign-exchange market; there was a period of fluctuation in exchange rates, which led to the introduction of the Exchange Equalization Account system whereby the authorities intervened not so much to maintain a given exchange rate as to moderate these fluctuations.

The era of the flexible exchange rates was also the era of world slump. It was a period of 'beggar my neighbour', a period when most of the old standards and aims of maintaining a solid currency appeared to have gone. Since employment would be increased by pushing exports up and keeping imports down there was a certain mad logic in undervaluing one's currency. World trade was dwindling, not because of any inherent difficulty over international liquidity, but because each country strove to limit its imports and increase its exports, and was prepared to face the possibility of a slight or a substantial undervaluation of its currency to achieve this. The climax perhaps came when the American Government arbitrarily changed the dollar price of gold, finally settling for a price of $35 per ounce against the previous $20. The devaluation was not prompted by a balance of payments crisis, or even particularly a desire to push exports, so much as to raise internal prices and stimulate business. It was an arbitrary act taken without regard to the effects on other economies, and, together with an accompanying change in the price of silver, caused a drain of these metals to the United States and results which ranged from inconvenient in the case of India to disastrous in the case of the silver-based Chinese economy.

It was a dismal period in world trade, and its psychological effects are still with us. Gradually, however, some measure of order was being restored. The U.S., which had boycotted the World Economic Conference in 1933, joined with the United Kingdom and France in the Tripartite Agreement of 1936, which attempted to regulate the throat-cutting competition in exchange depreciation, and the main currencies, while free to fluctuate, in practice settled down to an acceptable exchange rate which lasted until the beginning of the Second World War.

One of the important consequences of this dismal period was the dislike for flexible exchange rates which became a marked feature of the wartime and postwar discussions. It must, in all fairness, be pointed out that most of the problems of the period arose not so much from flexible exchange rates as from the completely self-centred actions of various governments who were prepared to protect their own national interests by a blatant disregard of the effects of their actions on others. The consequences were of course that all suffered, but the big and the strong suffered less than the poor or weak nations. The self-centred attitude of the United States has been remarked upon. But American behaviour was no worse than that of most nations – it was only her size and economic power that made these actions so much more momentous. Raising the price of silver was merely a political move to gain the administration the votes of the silver-mining states and to create employment there, and this the Silver Purchase Act did. The fact that the move virtually wrecked the Chinese currency implied no hostility or ill-will to that country. It merely implied indifference – and in many respects that was more unforgivable.

This was of course a passing phase. But when it passed, the odium stuck to one aspect, that of the flexible exchange rate: rightly or wrongly this method of adjustment was condemned, and this problem of liquidity was bound to reappear in the post-war world.

The negotiations for a postwar structure started during the war, and the decisions were coloured by the prewar experience. Unfortunately this background experience did not prove to be particularly relevant in the postwar era.

Although past experience was uppermost in the minds of those negotiating, what had changed was the nations' attitude towards cooperation. The two main trading nations who during the war were in a position to formulate the postwar rules were the United States and Britain. Both had experienced a profound change of heart.

It has sometimes been remarked that the most fervent advocate of total abstinence is the reformed drunk. It is difficult to examine the American attitude without feeling that their enthusiastic condemnation of the deplorable practices of the prewar period was in part at least a condemnation of their own rather sterile attitude of those days. This reformation did not of course inhibit them from detecting the mote in the eye of another with rather more alacrity than charity.

The American administration approached the problem of reforming the errors of the prewar years in a spirit of new-found enthusiasm, and a consciousness that, during the first few years of peace, they would be the dominant nation in the international economic scene. Though Britain was a wartime ally they felt that the attitude of the British Government in the prewar period was almost as culpable as that of Nazi Germany. A conscious feeling that British imperialism rather than Communism would be the arch-enemy of world peace appears to have dominated American thought at this time. The American attitude to the Sterling Area system was fairly simple. It was a discriminatory system designed to protect markets for Britain, and thus exclude American competitors. It was backed by a pernicious system of preferences, and in an ideal world these would be swept away. The war had given an unrivalled opportunity, as it seemed, to break up the system. The terms of Lend Lease were somewhat ambiguous. But the Americans interpreted them, not merely as excluding the United Kingdom from virtually every South American market, but as conditional upon the ending of Imperial Preference and the abolition of the Sterling Area. The American Government was now supplying much war material free under Lend Lease, but was simultaneously anxious to acquire much of the re-mainder of Britain's vastly depleted gold and foreign-currency reserves, in order to make Britain the more amenable to American ideas; and a grim, if unpublicized, struggle seems to have taken place. In this the British Government was remarkably successful, but it was fairly clear that success must ultimately lie with the Americans. The longer the war continued the weaker the British position became, and it was inevitable that American ideas would dictate the postwar system.

So far as Britain was concerned, the dominant figure in the negotiations was Lord Keynes, whose criticisms of the follies of the British prewar policy had been so triumphantly vindicated. Keynes and his team were determined that at all costs there would be no return to the massive unemployment of the past. If a policy of full employment were to bring about a temporary balance of payments crisis, this must be averted by some means other than the old discredited policy of cutting employment.

World liquidity, in other words, must be created on a massive scale so that no country need accept unemployment to cure such a crisis, but would instead be able to draw automatically and massively on reserves furnished by a Clearing Union.

What would create difficulties in international liquidity would be a persistent imbalance of trade which would cause the creditor nation gradually to drain off reserves from the debtor. The latter had an obvious incentive to cure this drain; Keynes's most original idea was the concept that the persistent creditor as well as the debtor would be penalized, in that it would be required to meet interest charges.

The Clearing Union, a sort of central bank which would hold stocks of an international currency, would have very large assets, and would levy charges both on persistent creditors and debtors. But access to it would be virtually automatic.

It was not a suggestion that was likely to appeal to the American Government. The Americans were aware that they would in all probability be extensive creditors in the postwar years, as they had been in the prewar period, and they regarded such a credit as a sign of virtue, rather than something to be penalized. The American administration was moreover moving from a rather idealistic New Deal attitude, albeit an idealism which had rarely been reflected in their approach to international economic problems, to a more conservative frame of mind which was likely to make them even less receptive to imaginative postwar plans.

America's alternative plan, the White Plan, makes sense only if it is appreciated that her attitude was becoming progressively more cautious. There were in a sense not one but several White Plans, each more cautious than the one before. The original drafts had been almost as imaginative as Keynes's plan. The authorized version was a sadly watered-down affair which contemplated an international fund of some $5 billion, but which in its effects appeared to be designed to limit American commitments rather than to solve the problems of international liquidity and freer international trade, which had been the original aims.

The International Monetary Fund

The International Monetary Fund, or I.M.F. as it is commonly called, emerged from the Bretton Woods Conference of 1944; in essence it reflected the American White Plan, with the odd, and usually minor, amendment in deference to Keynes's alternative plan.

It consists essentially of a fund of members' currencies, together with gold, and the essential principle on which it operates is that in times of difficulty members may buy gold or foreign currencies from the Fund, using their own currencies to purchase whatever other currency they require. Sometimes the term 'loan' is rather inaccurately used. Strictly speaking the Fund does not lend currencies but only sells them against other currencies.

Thus if the United Kingdom found herself, during a balance of payments crisis, short of American dollars, she might purchase them from the Fund. The total assets of the Fund would remain unchanged by the purchase but its composition would have altered in that the supply of sterling would have risen, while the supply of dollars would have fallen.

Each member on joining is given a quota, the amount of its contribution to the Fund. This quota is determined by the member's relative importance in world trade, and in turn determines its drawing rights and voting rights on the administration of the Fund. The quota is paid partly in gold or dollars, and partly in the member's own currency.

The conditions under which a nation may purchase gold or foreign currencies depend largely on the extent to which the Fund has already accumulated the currency in question. The first 'tranche' (i.e. 'slice') – twenty-five per cent of a member's quota, representing generally its gold contribution – is available almost automatically: so too is the next twenty-five per cent, provided the I.M.F. is satisfied that some efforts are being made by the nation concerned to deal with the balance of payments problem. For each successive 'tranche' up to 200 per cent of the quota, the conditions under which the Fund will sell currencies become increasingly more severe, and the rate of interest charged gets higher.

It was hoped that the I.M.F. would act as a clearing house, so that if a nation were paying in its own currency to purchase another currency, a third nation might simultaneously be interested in purchasing the currency of the original 'borrower'. This would of course reduce the surplus of the original 'borrower's' currency; and such a multilateral clearing system would also economize in the size of the balances involved. In fact, as we shall see, the I.M.F. has tended to be subjected to unilateral demands for one currency at a time. There do not appear to have been any significant instances of the same currency being bought and sold more or less simultaneously.

A nation is of course under pressure to restore the *status quo* by repurchasing within a limited time any excess of its own currency, and this is a condition of purchasing. In addition interest charges have to be met. The rules, fortunately, have been interpreted with a fair amount of discretion, especially where underdeveloped countries have been concerned.

The aim of the Fund was to encourage multilateral trade and increase world liquidity, thus obviating the need to indulge either in the competitive depreciation of currencies or in currency discrimination. To this end a member nation, on joining, has to declare the par value of its currency in gold or U.S. dollars, and undertakes to try to maintain this value unaltered. In addition, after a transitional postwar period, which proved to be remarkably permanent, member nations were to permit free convertibility on current account, although controls on movements of capital between countries were still to be permissible.

The Fund has in practice accepted the values of currencies declared by member nations, although it was presumably open to the Fund to object to values as being unrealistic. Once fixed, the par values cannot be altered by more than ten per cent except with the approval of the Fund.

This provision has not been particularly successful. If a nation contemplates devaluation, there is an excellent case for being 'bloody, bold and resolute'. Devaluation is always an upsetting action, and a small devaluation is in many ways more unsettling than a large one. Devaluation is a drastic expedient, and a small devaluation is liable to be regarded as a harbinger of more trouble, while a large devaluation at least convinces speculators that another cut in value is highly unlikely. A devaluation of less than ten per cent is not therefore likely to cure any problem. The British devaluation of September 1949 was about thirty per cent.

On the other hand a devaluation of more than ten per cent, if it is to be successful, has to be carried out with the maximum of speed and advance secrecy. Extensive consultation beforehand with the I.M.F. would be highly risky if the currency has any international standing whatsoever. Most devaluations made by I.M.F. members have in theory observed the conventions, but the amount of say that the I.M.F. has really had has been small, and the Fund has in most cases accepted a *fait accompli*.

If the problem of devaluation procedures has not been fully solved, progress towards convertibility has been almost as difficult. In part this has been a failure of the I.M.F., but it is in part due to the reluctance of member nations to give up the practices which served so well in time of trouble.

Keynes foresaw that it would be difficult to persuade the persistent creditor nation to take as active an interest in curing an imbalance of payments as the persistent debtor, and he had for that reason attempted to 'fine' the creditor as well as the debtor by interest charges. The American Government would have none of this, predicting correctly that for years to come the American economy would be in credit. As a gesture – it was no more – a 'scarce currency' clause was written into the I.M.F. Charter permitting discrimination against a currency which was persistently in short supply. As it happened there was quite clearly a dollar shortage, indeed an acute dollar shortage, for some ten years after the opening of the Fund, but at no time was the scarce currency clause invoked, for at no time was the Fund so short of dollars as to make their scarcity an official fact.

The Fund, then, began its life with inadequate resources and unrealistic provisions: that it survived at all was due to the speed with which the Americans, who had so large a responsibility for the shape of the Fund, were prepared to modify their attitude when the true facts of the international economy were revealed by the crisis of 1947.

The inauguration of the Fund coincided with the drain on sterling caused by the premature return to convertibility. The lesson was clear. Not only was sterling immensely weakened but the whole world outside the U.S.A. was desperately short of dollars. As a means of dealing with the dollar shortage the I.M.F. was ludicrously inadequate. The United States stepped in with a massive injection of dollar aid through the Marshall Plan, and the I.M.F. quietly closed its doors again so far as Europe was concerned for several years, ruling that a country in receipt of Marshall Aid should not require the services of the Fund, save in very exceptional circumstances.

The Fund was at a very low level of activity for the next few years. The experiences of the late 1940s had indicated its limitations in dealing with really large-scale crises. During this period, in 1952, a stand-by system was inaugurated whereby the Fund could make an advance commitment to a nation which had some reason to anticipate a crisis, but did not wish actually to draw funds, until and unless absolutely necessary. The stand-by arrangements meant that a line of defence could be planned against the onset of a crisis, but at cheaper rates of interest than would have to be paid if the money was actually drawn.

In the early years, however, little was made of the stand-by provisions and it was not until 1956 that they were extensively used. In that year a new phase began with the appointment of a new director, and with the economic aftermath of the Suez crisis, when the United Kingdom and France had recourse to fairly large-scale borrowing.

During the sterling crises of 1957, the United Kingdom made extensive use of drawing rights and stand-by arrangements.

The revived activity of the I.M.F. brought into prominence the main criticism which could, all along, be levelled at it: the comparative smallness of its resources – some $8 billion. Unfortunately too this figure gave an exaggerated picture of its true resources, for it now became painfully obvious that very few currencies were actively sought by potential borrowers, and large amounts of the I.M.F. reserves, being in currencies which nobody was evincing any desire to borrow, were reserves for book-keeping purposes only. They formed the basis of some members' claims to drawing rights, but added virtually nothing to the resources of the Fund.

The situation was complicated by the fact that international trade had expanded since the inception of the Fund, thus increasing the need for reserves of international liquidity. In 1958 therefore the I.M.F. agreed to raise quotas by some fifty per cent and, in the case of some nations like West Germany whose trading role had increased dramatically, to increase the size of their quotas. By these means the Fund's quotas had been raised to nearly $15 billion by the next year or two; although this merely meant that the Fund was keeping pace with the growth of international trade, and not that it was as yet playing a greater role than that originally envisaged for it.

The Fund has continued to expand its activities slowly, not so much in the massive lending of funds, but as a clearing house for advice. In the process, perhaps, America's influence on the I.M.F. has diminished – the Fund may be on its way to achieving real international status, but the limitations imposed by its still inadequate quotas, a legacy of American opinion in the early 1940s, is still the greatest handicap to its emergence as a true central bank for the whole world.

The most immediate prospects for advance in I.M.F. activities seem to be in the increasingly flexible approach to problems of lending. In recent years the conditions under which quota rights can be taken up have been relaxed, especially for the underdeveloped countries. It is quite possible that a greater degree of automatic access to the Fund's resources, coupled with a longer period of repayment, might encourage more nations to regard their drawing rights with the Fund as part of their reserves. In this way – the back door so to speak – the principle of virtually automatic access to the Fund, which Lord Keynes enunciated twenty years before when the I.M.F. was being set up, may be achieved. If Britain were enabled to treat her quota rights as part of her currency reserves, the British monetary authorities could accept with equanimity the possibility of greater fluctuations in their reserves without feeling obliged to introduce a credit squeeze whenever they dropped by £50–100 million: any move towards this would make a coherent policy of expansion a much easier aim.

Ad hoc *arrangements*

Early in 1962 a further, if somewhat *ad hoc*, arrangement was made which applied to ten I.M.F. members who played a leading role in world trade. These countries agreed under certain conditions to make supplementary credits available to one another, but not to other members of the Fund; the total additional credits which would thus be available to add to the resources of the Fund would amount to another $6 billion. The fact that the members will lend only among themselves is not likely significantly to restrict the benefits of this expansion of credit, since any severe crisis which would strain the Fund's resources would probably originate in one of these countries. Indeed the arrangement is likely to increase the resources available to bolster up the key currencies of sterling and dollar, and the United Kingdom and the United States have probably most to gain from the new provisions of this so-called 'Paris Club', or 'Group of Ten'.

In addition the central banks of the leading trading nations have in recent years concluded a number of 'swap' arrangements whereby they agree in times of crisis to accumulate each others' currencies. This temporarily 'sterilizes' considerable quantities of a currency which is under pressure, and so can stall off a crisis.

The sources of international liquidity

That the I.M.F. has proved to be rather inadequate to its task of maintaining world liquidity at a satisfactory level is difficult to dispute. But there has as yet been no decisive failure in world liquidity. The machinery, inadequate as it has been, has nevertheless functioned. Why then should it not continue to do so in the middle 1960s?

The fact that the inadequate arrangements functioned through-out the 1940s, 1950s and early 1960s is possibly due to three events which are in their way unique, and which are highly un-likely to recur, at least in the foreseeable future. They represented a process whereby one or the other of the key currencies became available on a fairly massive scale during this period, and so were able to supplement international reserves. The key currencies were of course the dollar and sterling.

The massive dollar aid under the Marshall Plan meant that from about 1947 to 1952 a vast amount of this key currency was appearing in the foreign reserves of many countries on a scale which would have been quite impossible by way of ordinary trade. Even when this aid began to dry up there was a continuing, if minor, flow of American military aid and American military expenditure, which provided a useful supplement.

As this dollar source was drying up, a more modest, but none the less useful, source which had been developing as early as 1947 began to assume respectable proportions. This was the release of the blocked sterling balances accumulated during the war by the Commonwealth countries, the Middle Eastern countries, and to a lesser extent South America. These had of course been blocked at the time of the sterling convertibility experiment of July 1947, but by the early 1950s they were released on a fairly generous basis, giving those countries which chose to hold reserves in sterling an opportunity to amass this key currency.

By the middle 1950s this source too was drying up, and the only substantial remnant was probably the Egyptian account, which was in any event reblocked at the time of the Suez crisis. For a year or two there was no substantial increase of international liquidity by non-recurring means, apart from the growing American overseas aid. By about 1958, however, the phenomenon of the weakening dollar began to appear. The Americans were beginning to experience a deficit in their balance of payments, which was in time to reduce substantially their holdings of gold and even give rise to speculation about an American devaluation via a rise in the price of gold.

While this situation was embarrassing for the Americans it was not in its early years dangerous, and so far as the rest of the world was concerned the redistribution of the world gold stocks made their currency-reserve problems a good deal easier. But all this time, the American deficit was being caused by the policy of massive overseas spending and aid: it did not arise because America could not pay her way by trade. The continuation of this state of affairs depended on two assumptions, neither of which was likely to pass unchallenged in the mid-1960s.

The first of these was that the U.S. Government could and would tolerate a continuing drain of dollars. If the Americans pushed up the level of their exports faster than their imports or if they cut foreign aid and overseas spending, then the bonanza would be over. By the middle 1960s the situation looked like occurring; disillusion about the effects of American aid, a lessening of tension in Europe, and a reformulation of American strategy which was likely to cut overseas spending meant that an automatic increase in the dollar holdings would not necessarily continue.

The second assumption was that the dollar would continue to be regarded as being as good as gold by those nations whose reserves were increasing. In 1964 and even more in 1965 France looked like challenging this assumption, for she chose to exercise her right to convert her extensive dollar holdings into gold – possibly as much as $400 million in 1964, and possibly half as much again in 1965. Her example was not immediately followed by the other main holders of dollars, but the effect was to throw a good deal of doubt on the whole principle of the key-currency system.

Thus it was that, by the middle 1960s, the era when the world liquidity problem could be met by relying on the two key currencies, the dollar and sterling, appeared to be passing. There was no reason to suppose that there would be a massive flight from the two key currencies, but it was clear that their usefulness was limited. A further expansion of world trade would depend largely on another solution to the problem. Some of the possible solutions we must now examine.

Raising the price of gold

Gold has always held a place of special esteem in men's hearts, and it was for long the central pivot of the currency of any self-respecting nation. Even when it was finally displaced in its internal use for currency backing, its role as the chief source of world liquidity, the chief and best form of external reserve, remained for a long time unchallenged. But the decline in the role of gold after the end of the Second World War was marked. The fact that this decline coincided with the appearance of fresh problems of international liquidity has not gone unremarked, and there is a powerful school of thought which argues that the decline of gold was a substantial cause of the world liquidity problem.

For the obvious factor is that gold has lost value. Its official price, which is most widely known in American terms as $35 per fine ounce, has remained unchanged since 1934. But during and after the Second World War, the dollar, like all the other main currencies, was subject to inflation, and its purchasing power now is probably less than half what it was before the war. Putting it another way, if gold were to have the same purchasing power as in 1934, its price would have to be altered from $35 to $70 or even $100 per ounce.

At the moment the known gold stocks of the world outside the Soviet bloc are about $40 billion. The world supply of gold is growing by about two to three per cent per annum, but the increases in foreign-reserve holdings amount only to about half this. Here then in a nutshell is the problem. If liquidity depends on the supply of gold and trade is increasing faster than the gold reserves (i.e. faster than one to two per cent per annum) then there is at least a potential problem.

There are a number of qualifications, however. Firstly, as we have seen, we need not accept the proposition that only gold will increase world liquidity. Secondly we need not assume that only a fraction of the gold becomes available for foreign reserves. Much of the rest is used for industrial and commercial use; and an unknown, but almost certainly vast, quantity is absorbed in the apparently insatiable markets of Asia, especially India and

Pakistan, where it is much prized for personal wealth and adornment, and as a hedge against a distrusted currency, against which it may sell unofficially and illegally at several times its official price. If it were possible for Asian governments to end this massive gold hoarding by individuals, not only the difficulties of their countries, but also the problem of world liquidity, would be vastly simplified.

No solution to the problem of gold hoarding is in sight, however; and, in the absence of any better and more widely acceptable method of increasing world liquidity, the possibility of raising the price of gold must be considered. The figures $50, $70 or $100 per ounce have been proposed, as being more realistic than the present price.

The result of raising the price, it has been argued, would be twofold. At one stroke it would double or treble the value of existing stocks and so go a very long way to meet the problem of inadequate reserves. In addition it would encourage the reopening of a considerable number of marginal mines and ensure that a greater supply of gold reached the world market each year.

If these results were indeed possible then the case for revaluing would be cogent. But in spite of these manifest advantages, the weight of informed opinion is, if anything, on the side of the *status quo*.

In examining the objections it is worth noting that there are two methods by which revaluation would be possible. Either the U.S. could alter the dollar price on its own decision, knowing that the weight of its economy could compel other nations to follow suit; or the revaluation could be decided by a conference of all the leading nations.

The first method would in fact be a unilateral devaluation of the dollar, with all the economic and political consequences that such a move would imply. America's creditors would find that a proportion of their debts had been in effect repudiated. Those central banks which held dollars as part of their reserves would find that the value had been effectively reduced. The fact that they too would probably be forced to devalue to the same extent would hardly lessen their disgruntlement. These disadvantages might to some extent be avoided if some form of recompense, a gold guarantee, were to operate. But the political, and even more the practical, problems of deciding which debts were domestic and which were non-resident – which were to be compensated and which were not – could be complex.

The alternative approach to revaluation might be by mutual agreement among the leading nations, possibly as a consequence of an international agreement. This would ensure that the obloquy did not fall on the United States alone. But the practical problems would be enormous. The proportion of gold to foreign currencies held by central banks as reserves, varies considerably, from well over ninety per cent in the case of the Bank of England to about thirty per cent elsewhere. If it became clear that a conference, at which those attending would be representatives of central banks, was even contemplating revaluing gold upwards – and by implication devaluing all national currencies – then the effect on the existing currency reserves would be profound. There would be a concerted effort to get rid of accumulated holdings of such currencies as the dollar and sterling. Whatever the *ultimate* effect of revaluing gold, the *immediate* effect would be a profound currency crisis: overnight the major currencies of the world would become virtually unacceptable, and in consequence liquidity would be drastically reduced, rather than increased.

Quite apart from these disastrous effects on foreign currency, there would be an obvious tendency towards inflation. Those countries which had been fortunate enough in the scramble to acquire gold or convert existing currency reserves into gold could find their reserves instantly doubled or trebled, with no sacrifice needed on their own part. They would then face the temptation to use their new-found wealth in a politically popular spending spree.

Last but not least of the ill effects would be the unfair distribution of good fortune. A nation which had acted as a good world citizen by accepting foreign currencies as a reserve, literally at their face value, would lose: a nation which had hoarded gold, and followed a generally dog-in-the-manger attitude would gain; and among the obvious beneficiaries from the revaluation would be the chief gold producers, countries like South Africa or the Soviet Union, which on political grounds alone the United States, the ultimate arbiter of the price of gold, would be least likely to wish to assist.

It might thus appear that the arguments against raising the price of gold are so overwhelming, that the policy could be ruled out. But it would be a bold man who committed himself to an unequivocal statement that gold will not be revalued. For although the revaluation of gold is not the best solution to the problem of world liquidity, it may turn out to be the only practicable one. Other solutions, discussed later, which depend on more sophisticated policies in the form of the creation of international credits, are obviously rather more difficult to agree upon and to operate in the present state of international relations. If, through the I.M.F. or any other international organization, an acceptable alternative is found, it will be a triumph for the forces of common sense and goodwill among the nations: but it would be sanguine to expect that, merely because there is a sound case for creating international credits, automatically they will be created. If all else fails then the revaluation of gold may have to be the solution, with the I.M.F. seeking methods of limiting the ill effects. For it is already clear that a number of leading economists are at least open to the arguments for revaluing, not because they regard this as the best solution, but rather as the best *practical* solution in an imperfect world.

The gold pool – its rise and fall

An interesting example of cooperation among the central banks of some of the leading trading nations within the past few years was the creation on an unofficial basis of a 'gold pool'. The arrangement, which started in 1961, was initially concerned with holding the price of gold fairly steady during a crisis, by the formation of a ring or sales consortium of central banks which would share the burden of offering gold for sale on the London gold market. Each central bank was given a quota of gold which it had to provide for sale. Thus, for example, the main burden of supplying gold would not necessarily fall on the Federal Reserve Bank of New York, if the dollar happened to be under pressure. Any gold thus provided and sold, could be repurchased when the crisis was over and distributed among the central banks again.

Subsequently the system was adapted to deal with situations where the price of gold was tending to fall below the American price of $35. When gold was available in the London market at or below the official American selling price (i.e. the price at which an American Federal Reserve Bank would sell to another central bank), the Bank of England would purchase gold on the market on behalf of all members of the pool. The gold thus acquired would be distributed among member nations.

The pool began to operate as a buying consortium in 1962 and fairly rapidly bought some $80 million of gold; this was providentially available when the price of gold again began to rise, and helped to stabilize the position. The Cuban crisis in October caused an unprecedented panic demand for gold, and the sales consortium reappeared to share the burden of supplying it. Subsequently, as the crisis passed, the same consortium was able to repurchase all the gold it had sold.

Thus there had been established, on an unofficial basis, the machinery for a selling consortium which could be put into operation in a crisis, and a buying consortium which was able to acquire gold at a relatively low price by coordination among the central banks. The participating central banks not only increased their cooperation but in the event made something of a modest profit by their intervention on the London gold market.

The pool might be seen, at its most favourable, as a sort of international exchange equalization scheme, where the central banks by coordinating their buying or selling policies were able to hold the London gold market price at about the level at which the Federal Reserve authorities are required to sell gold to other central banks.

The gold pool worked satisfactorily as long as in the long run its sales were are least balanced by purchases – otherwise it would serve merely as a means of spreading the loss of gold among the central banks if one of their currencies was under attack. After

1964 this in effect happened, as more and more holders of dollar securities apparently preferred to hold gold. The demand thus created was only in part borne immediately by the U.S. reserves, since half the gold supplied to the gold markets via the gold pool came from the non-American members.

France withdrew in 1967, and the American commitment was increased accordingly; but demand for gold soared after the British devaluation in November of that year triggered off a fresh run on the dollar. In three months the gold pool appears to have supplied nearly $2,000 million with no prospects of being able to buy back. In a dramatic move the central banks ended the gold pool and their commitments to supply the London gold market, and a two-tier gold price arose – the official $35 price for trans-actions between central banks and a free price for gold, which was, however, no longer supplied from central bank sources.

Flexible exchange rates

One reason why so much liquidity is required to further inter-national trade is that it is always rather more expensive to defend a fixed exchange rate than one which is permitted to vary. The gold standard was such a fixed-exchange-rate system, although one which did not have to be consciously defended. The 'gold points' represented the limits within which the exchange rate could in practice vary. Similarly the present exchange-rate system under I.M.F. rules is a fixed position, in the sense that where the par value of £1 = $2.40, the Exchange Equalization Account will be operated to prevent the value of £1 rising above $2.42 or falling below $2.38. There is no particular difficulty in holding the value below $2.42 so long as the Exchange Equalization Account is prepared to pile up gold and foreign currency reserves, and this situation has never preoccupied the British Government for long. But the need to prevent the value of sterling falling below $2.32 is much more serious. Persistent pressure against sterling would have to be met by persistent selling of gold or foreign currencies by the Account, and when its resources, and even drawing rights from the I.M.F. and other aid, are limited, the monetary authorities must at times have wished that they had the power to permit a further fall in the value of sterling (which would, of course, violate the contractual rights incurred by I.M.F. membership to protect a fixed par value like $2.40).

This in brief is the case for the flexible exchange rate, the concept of allowing supply and demand to fix the value of a currency at any time so that the rate varies at will. This was, of course, the situation in the early 1930s, and the task of the Exchange Equalization Account was to iron out the wilder fluctuations, not to fix a particular value for sterling.

There is thus a good deal to be said for the idea of a flexible exchange rate. Its most obvious value in the present context is that it resolves many of the problems of international liquidity, in that the reserves which each country at present feels it must hold can be substantially reduced once the necessity to defend a fixed position is gone.

We may find ourselves in very deep water if we try to estimate what the par value of each currency ought to be so that the purchasing power of money, in any currency whatsoever, is more or less the same throughout the world. If a country attempts to define a par value which cannot automatically be tested by the right to use gold instead, then the actual purchasing power may be considerably different from the legal value, as we have already seen. A government may make a wrong estimate when it fixes a par value: even if its judgement is correct at the time, degrees of inflation or deflation differing from those which prevail outside the country may render the original par value irrelevant. Moreover, a government may have its own economic or political motives for undervaluing or overvaluing its own currency – reasons which may seem good and proper for its own national interests but which distort the pattern of international transactions.

All these problems are avoided, in theory at least, by permitting exchange rates to find their own level. The Exchange Equalization Account or its equivalent has a rather easier task, simply confining very erratic movements, and not protecting a particular value.

In many respects the arguments for the flexible exchange rate system since the end of the Second World War have been persuasive. The main internal economic problem in most countries has been to avoid inflation, rather than to cure depression, and the danger has been excessive rather than inadequate demand. What can a government do to cure excessive demand once it has appeared? Some form of deflation may be necessary, although this is politically an unpopular course. The ideal solution might be to reduce demand by reducing incomes: in monetary terms this is exceedingly difficult. The practical opposition to wage-cuts is immense, and it is a solution which most governments would rather avoid.

So far as the external problems of inflation are concerned, there is a strong case for allowing a certain amount of depreciation. If the exchange rate falls, some internal prices – mainly those affected substantially by import prices – and the volume of exports may rise: thus there has effectively been a reduction in real wages and income in a community although money wages have not fallen. Money simply buys less. This is merely an acceptance of an inflationary situation.

There are a number of snags to this argument. Inflation even when unchecked tends to cure itself eventually at a new level, and with a redistribution of national income; and the chief fault of such inflation may be the latter effect. Certain sections of the community may benefit at the expense of others. Thus to allow depreciation as a cure for a balance of payments problem could involve a redistribution of national wealth which might or might not be acceptable but which was certainly not deliberately intended.

A second argument against the use of depreciation is that it may go a good deal further than was intended. A variation of up to, say, ten per cent in exchange rates might be regarded as tolerable: a variation of fifty per cent might be regarded as quite disastrous. What would determine the extent of the change? Among other things there would be the problem of an 'absorption' effect. If the practice of depreciation were to be contained, then a rise in exports (itself inflationary) would have to be met by a cut in home expenditure – by the equivalent of deflationary policy. If home expenditure were not cut, depreciation would go on, exports would not rise readily, since in conditions of full employment potential exports could be absorbed in the home market, and inflation might not be checked until the exchange rate levelled out at a fraction of its former value. Thus one can say that, as a means of dealing with balance of payments difficulties, a policy of depreciation does not enable a government to avoid politically unpopular actions, like deflation, any more than it can under the present system. Depreciation under a flexible-exchange-rate system may be an answer, but it is not a painless answer.

It is possible that the insidious process, not of avoiding painful decisions on deflation, but of delaying them, and so possibly worsening the ultimate shock, is the greatest danger in the use of flexible exchange rates. If they are to be used and used legitimately then there is at least as great a need for firm government action to ensure that depreciation, if it has to be used, constitutes an instrument of adjustment to rectify an economic problem, and not a means of evading a solution for a time, by repudiation, or evasion of liabilities at home and abroad.

It is unfortunate too that the only period during which flexible exchange rates were prevalent, the 1930s, was also the period of some of the worst excesses of 'beggar my neighbour' policies, with strong nations attempting to cure their own internal problems by actions which could not but worsen the position of their neighbours, and even more of the poor or weak nations. The chief evil of the situation in the 1930s was not the flexible-exchange-rate system itself so much as the tendency of some nations deliberately to undervalue their currencies in order to cheapen their exports and increase the price of imports, thus exporting unemployment – a typical 'beggar my neighbour' policy of the period.

The record of none of the larger nations during this period is particularly good, and the introduction of the I.M.F. system, whatever its faults, represented an enormous advance in international behaviour. Unfortunately it led to a blanket condemnation, rather than a selective disapproval, of the practices of the 1930s.

The attitude of nations or individuals to any way of solving a problem is inevitably conditioned by history and experience, as much as by the merits of the particular solution. The fairly unanimous desire among many of the leading nations to end the unsatisfactory trading system, and the growing economic self-sufficiency – in fact the whole 'beggar my neighbour' attitude – of the 1930s led to the repudiation of, among many other practices, the flexible-exchange-rate system, without too close an examination of whether it was as pernicious as some of the others.

This 'guilt by association' has persisted, although less strongly, and it is perhaps too late to expect any substantial change in attitude. The Canadian Government has experimented with a flexible-exchange-rate system without ill effects either to its own economy or to its trading partners. The advocates of flexible exchange rates include some highly distinguished economists. Here again, as with the price of gold, the end-solution may not be perfect, but it is, in the light of history, the most acceptable – and there is little evidence that the experience of the 1930s has been forgotten.

A compromise solution?

The very considerable merit in the flexible-exchange-rate system, so far as a nation like Britain is concerned, is that it makes it possible to economize in gold and currency reserves by ending the necessity to defend a particular value. There is at least a case for arguing that it would be possible to permit a larger variation in the par points. Instead of being obliged to maintain a par value within the range £1 = $2.38 to £1 = 2.42, it might be easier to sustain any strain if the outer limits were altered to £1 = $2.35 to £1 = $2.45. The $2.45 limit would of course be academic, since it would be the $2.35 limit that gave a measure of relief to the Exchange Equalization Account. On the other hand, to fix the range at between $2.35 and $2.42 would invite the conclusion that the par value was acceptable at $2.38·5 – and whatever case there might be for devaluation, a one and a half per cent devaluation would be quite pointless, disturbing confidence without having any effective consequences.

The idea of a floating exchange rate of this type has certain merits – and in a sense is a compromise. Certain of the monetary agreements concluded in Europe in the 1960s may in time lead in this direction.

Other solutions

During the early 1960s a number of alternative plans have been mooted which would enable world liquidity to be substantially increased within the framework of a revised I.M.F. Before considering in outline some of these proposals, it is worth repeating what the problem is, and how it is being tackled at the moment.

Basically the problem is that there is no satisfactory international currency which can be regarded as a generally acceptable reserve and whose quantity could conveniently be altered to meet the changing level of world trade. Because of the inadequate supplies of the only currency hitherto completely acceptable – gold – sterling and latterly the dollar have been used as a supplement. Not only do these currencies have certain inadequacies but the fact that they are national currencies first, and international currencies, in a sense, by default, means that there is always a grave danger that international liquidity problems will be subordinated to the national economic problems of the two countries whose currencies are involved – or alternatively, as has happened in the past with Britain, that national economic objectives will be frustrated by the demands of maintaining sterling as an international currency.

The dollar is by now more important than sterling as a reserve currency. By 1958, rather more than half the foreign-currency reserves of the world were in the form of dollar holdings, with sterling virtually representing the rest – the bulk of the sterling holders being the Sterling Area countries. Of course gold was still far and away the most important form of reserve holdings, but the role of the currencies, particularly the dollar, was growing, and sterling was more or less holding its own in absolute if not in relative terms.

The gold reserves of the central banks of the nations have been growing at about two per cent annually since the end of the war, even allowing for the falling away in recent years. World trade has been growing at two or three times that rate. As we have seen, the potential deficiency in world liquidity has been avoided by rather fortuitous releases of sterling or dollars, and the present source of increases in liquidity has been the deficit in the American balance of payments, which in the late 1950s and early 1960s varied between $1·5 and 2 billion annually. As long as the American Government is prepared to accept this state of affairs the world-liquidity problem can be staved off, at the expense of creating difficulties for the U.S. Treasury. But the American Government need not, and indeed, cannot, accept such a solution indefinitely.

It need not accept it in the sense that the American deficit is not in its current account (i.e. it does not represent an inability to pay its way in the world). The deficit arises on the capital account, on the level of American military expenditure overseas, and its gifts, loans and investments in other countries. A cut in such expenditure might have unfortunate consequences, but in most cases these would not have to be borne by the Americans themselves. A change in government, or in the mood of the American taxpayer, might cause a revulsion towards what must sometimes seem an endless drain of American money and resources to an ungrateful world. A comparatively small change in American policy, or even a comparatively small increase in the efficiency of American productive methods, might either end this capital deficit, or further increase the current surplus to such a point that this persistent addition to world reserves outside the U.S.A. abruptly dried up.

So far the American Government has avoided any precipitate action which would solve its own problem at the expense of worsening the world liquidity position. But even the United States cannot support the massive drain of gold and dollars indefinitely. The U.S. Gold Reserves have fallen from a high peak of $25 billion in 1945 to about $10 billion in early 1968. Of this nearly $14 billion is required for statutory purposes, and the remainder is not likely to last indefinitely. The practical consequences of a continued gold drain on this scale was that the American Government would have to halt the drain even at the expense of very severe currency or trade controls. Whatever the political or economic consequences, it was certain as a political necessity that no American administration would tolerate a continued gold drain. Thus, however the problem is tackled, the immediate consequence of an American move to rectify the unbalance in its capital account will be an aggravation of the liquidity problem for the rest of the world.

What then are the alternatives? They can be divided into two types – those which supplement the I.M.F. facilities and those which would involve altering the structure of the I.M.F. The former are, of course, a good deal easier to implement, and to a degree some of them have already been invoked with greater or less effect, as we have indicated.

The first possibility is to broaden the exchange standard. At present the only two currencies which are at all widely used as reserves are of course the dollar and sterling. What other currencies might be used? Those which immediately spring to mind are the Swiss franc, the West German Deutschmark or in recent years the French franc. Indeed there is every prospect that the currencies of the Common Market will assume an increasing importance. But there are some limitations to this principle of broadening the base. Some of the most desirable currencies, the Swiss franc for example, could never make more than a marginal contribution since the economies on which they are based are too small to serve as international bankers on a world scale; and equally important is the possibility that a country whose currency was widely held as reserves elsewhere might in turn attempt to accumulate other currencies as a defensive measure – a step which is not likely to promote world liquidity. It is not impossible to envisage a situation where Italy might accumulate Deutschmarks to offset a large holding of lire by Germany, while Germany might by similar reasoning strive desperately to acquire lire to offset Italian holdings of Deutschmarks.

The dual system of sterling and dollars has a number of disadvantages. Speculation against sterling immediately strengthens the dollar and vice versa. Whether the solution of using more than two currencies would improve or worsen matters it is difficult to say. But certainly any nation which permitted its currency to be extensively used as an international reserve currency would experience some of the disadvantages from which the British economy has suffered in the postwar period.

Certainly, however, if the Common Market, whether or not enlarged by eventual British entry, is successful, then the economic super-power thus created will ultimately find itself with a common currency of world repute. But such a development is at least a decade away and the problem of inadequate liquidity will probably have to be firmly tackled long before that.

An alternative approach which does not require any change in the I.M.F. constitution is increased cooperation between central banks, and the use of 'swap' arrangements. Central banks have interests in common which tend to outweigh their differences. If for example one currency is under so much pressure that devaluation becomes a possibility, then while the immediate consequence may be the strengthening of other currencies because of 'hot' money movements away from the threatened currency, the ultimate result of a devaluation of one currency is to increase the pressure for devaluation of others. A devaluation of the dollar would almost inevitably cause a devaluation of sterling and the other major currencies of the world. Thus there is every incentive for central banks to back each other by swap arrangements, whereby they will undertake automatically to give each other assistance when in difficulty, and if necessary to hold each others' currencies, instead of converting them immediately.

The most formal of these arrangements dates from 1961 when sterling was under some pressure and the upward revaluation of the Deutschmark seemed to presage further changes; the central banks of the main countries of Western Europe then agreed at Basle to give accommodation to each others' currencies. In effect the Basle Agreement was a system of short-term loans by central banks to one another, accompanied by undertakings to hold more of one anothers' currencies in a crisis than was normal practice. The provisions were invoked by the British authorities for a few months in 1961 and again in 1963 and 1964.

A more extensive arrangement under I.M.F. auspices was the so-called Paris Club, whereby ten leading nations agreed to extend credit facilities to one another over and above their I.M.F. quotas, to the extent of about $6 billion. Switzerland, though not an I.M.F. member, subsequently joined.

The joint resources which can be made available by such arrangements were dramatically illustrated in the massive sterling operation of November 1964, when no less than $3 billion of credits were raised through the major central banks of the western world, to help stop the run on sterling.

The second approach to the problem of increasing international liquidity lies in some form of amendment of the structure of the International Monetary Fund. There are numerous plans which have been put forward, and it would be rather exhausting to explore the entire gamut. There are perhaps four approaches which are particularly interesting.

The first of these has been put forward by the American Professor Triffin. The Triffin Plan starts from the proposition that the use of national currencies for international reserves is the cause of many of the shortcomings of the present system. An increase in international liquidity under the present key-currency system may involve an increase of sterling or dollar liabilities, and thus potential problems for the monetary authorities of the two nations concerned. Triffin envisages a return to the more spacious principles of the Keynes Clearing Union plan (which was rejected in favour of the American proposals in formulating the I.M.F. rules) but with the important qualification that certain built-in inflationary tendencies in the Clearing Union would be eliminated.

Some modifications of detail have been made since Triffin initially put forward his proposals, but briefly the original plan envisaged that each member country should be required to deposit twenty per cent of its reserves with the I.M.F., which would use the deposits to acquire interest-bearing bonds of national governments. The Fund, by a policy of buying or selling such securities, could increase or reduce the foreign-currency reserves of the central banks. If the need for greater liquidity arose the I.M.F. would increase its purchases of securities in the open market. The central bank of a country in which this operation took place would in time find itself in possession of I.M.F.-issued cheques, with which the sellers of the securities had been paid. These cheques would represent increased deposits by the central bank with the I.M.F. and would constitute an increase in the country's foreign reserves.

Normally the intention would be to increase world liquidity, but if this had to be decreased the I.M.F. could reverse the process by selling securities.

This system would create a relationship between the I.M.F. and the central banks of member countries analogous to that which exists between the Bank of England and the commercial banks. The Bank of England, by a similar system of 'open-market' operations in buying or selling British Government securities, and so increasing or diminishing the assets of the commercial banks, can determine the extent to which the commercial banks can create credits.

Lest this system of creating I.M.F.-backed reserves should prove too inflationary, Triffin envisaged that the rate at which the Fund would be allowed to expand monetary reserves would be limited to, say, five per cent per annum.

Moreover the Fund would be able to offer overdraft facilities to central banks in difficulty. In fact it would in many ways serve as a central bank for the central banks, though that analogy should not be pushed too far.

The result of the Triffin Plan would be that sterling and the dollar would cease to be regarded as second-best alternatives to gold as a reserve, and over a comparatively long period the liabilities of the U.K. and the U.S. represented by existing holdings would be gradually reduced.

Although the Triffin Plan is in certain respects a return to the Keynesian concept of a considerably increased Fund with fairly generous rights of access, in other respects it is a radical departure. The I.M.F. would become a supranational body and its influence on the policies of the national central banks would be paramount. It is precisely this supranational element which is likely to stick in the throats of many national governments, who would be most unwilling to hand over any powers and limit their freedom to pursue economic policies at home which might run counter to the policies of the I.M.F. Nevertheless the plan is certainly one of the most imaginative to emerge in the postwar era.

Dr Bernstein, a former Director of the I.M.F., has produced a number of proposals which might be regarded as either one or two plans for the amendment of the I.M.F. Precisely because they are amendments to, rather than a radical revision of, the I.M.F., they are possibly more acceptable. They are in a sense somewhat technical innovations, but among their effects would be provision for relaxing the circumstances under which borrowing rights could be used, a general increase in quotas, more particularly in the quotas of some of the more important trading nations, and the creation of a new unit of account purchaseable from the I.M.F. which would form a compulsory part of the exchange reserves of member countries and could thus constitute a gold equivalent unit.

Thirdly, mention should be made of the specifically British proposals incorporated in the Maudling Plan. Again, like the Bernstein Plan this was sketched out only in broad detail. Its general effect would have been to extend the credit facilities available to a nation experiencing temporary problems by allowing the I.M.F. to take up, in exchange for gold guarantee credit certificates, any surplus of that particular currency (probably sterling or dollars) which was appearing in the world markets. The plan was put forward at the I.M.F. annual meeting in 1962 but was extremely coldly received by the American delegates, who seem to have believed at the time that America's difficulties were on the point of being solved. Since then, however, the U.S. monetary authorities appear to have been rather chastened by the continuing deficit, and are probably more amenable to proposals of this nature than they were.

Possibly the most far-reaching, and certainly the most idealistic, of the plans for international monetary reform is that associated with the English banker-economist Maxwell Stamp. The Stamp Plan envisages that the I.M.F. should be empowered to issue $3,000 million of certificates to the less developed nations. These would be used in normal commercial transactions by the recipients when purchasing goods from other members of the I.M.F., and would in time pass into the central-bank reserves of the developed countries, who would then treat them as part of their foreign reserves. Provided that there was general acceptance of these credits by the developed members of the I.M.F., so that they would not only accept them from the underdeveloped nations, but would use them in normal clearing transactions between one another, they would probably not even require a gold guarantee.

The issue of these certificates would mean that liquidity could be increased rapidly. But the certificates themselves would represent financial obligations of underdeveloped countries to the I.M.F. which would not be readily saleable. Indeed they might never be paid off, and would represent in effect free gifts to the underdeveloped nations.

This plan is quite revolutionary, but if the principle were to be accepted it might solve, simultaneously, two of the most perplexing problems of our time – international liquidity, and the provision of aid to the hungry third of the world. The scepticism, indeed the suspicion, with which the proposals were received, especially among Common Market members, suggests that the immediate prospects of its acceptance are not great. But the growing plight of the underdeveloped nations (discussed in Chapter 7) may yet breathe life into such a scheme.

Conclusion

It is of course a good deal easier to detail the problems of international liquidity than to solve them. In so far as most of the measures now being adopted are no more than stop-gap, it is clear that any step involving a radical reform of the I.M.F. procedure is fraught with difficulties. The auspices under which the original I.M.F. was created were in a sense unique. Many of the countries taking part were not only allies in war, but were occupied, and the discussions were dominated by the two leading allies, Britain and America. The latter was clearly emerging as the economic and political giant of the postwar world, and to a very large degree her word was law.

The balance of power has clearly shifted, and America is no longer the unchallenged financial power of the West. Europe has re-emerged as one of the major financial centres with interests which are not necessarily identical to those of the United States.

Presumably any realistic plan would have to accommodate the differing views of the United States and Europe, the former favouring a solution which would strengthen the role of the Group of Ten and the latter concerned rather to bolster the role of the I.M.F., which it had done so much to create.

The compromise solution – some would say the interim solution – which emerged in the late 1960s were special drawing rights to reinforce existing quotas. In effect these rights would enable I.M.F. members to acquire foreign currencies from other members who were required to accept a certain proportion of these 'paper gold' deposits. The solution, while intended to add $9.5 billions to world reserves by 1973, eased the situation but, arguably, merely postponed rather than resolved the issues which had arisen.

Eurodollars

Within recent years international liquidity has been significantly increased by the appearance of a new financial market – the Eurodollar. The market and its function are exceedingly complex: there is indeed considerable dispute as to its exact origin and its present function, but the general outlines can be fairly readily understood.

Basically the Eurodollar market comprises the transactions which are carried out in Europe in dollars instead of local currencies, that is, the borrowing and lending of dollars by British and other European banks.

The origins of the Eurodollar system are indeed somewhat obscure, but there appear to have been two sources. The first of these has its origins in the Cold War. Eastern European banks, like Western banks, need financial contacts in other countries.

Many banks engaging in foreign-exchange transactions find it expedient to maintain accounts in other countries and in currencies other than their own. Thus a British bank will find that when transacting business involving French currencies it is convenient to have an account in a correspondent bank in France, which may be credited or debited with any French currency the bank acquires in the course of its business.

Eastern European banks require their correspondent banks in Western Europe. Equally it would be expedient for them to have such correspondent banks in the United States. In practice, however, several East European banks seem to have preferred that any American transactions be handled by West European, especially British, banks rather than American banks. Therefore they have made dollar deposits in British banks, and the British banks have thus to a limited extent operated in another currency than their own.

It has apparently been possible for British banks with these dollar deposits to make at least short-term advances to other clients who have required dollar facilities for short periods, provided of course that the British banks are able to offer these borrowing facilities at rates competitive with the more orthodox American sources of dollar loans.

The second origin of the Eurodollar market was the difference in interest rates prevailing in Europe and in the United States. In the first instance the rate of interest which could be paid in America to foreign holders of dollars was limited by federal statute, and during the late 1950s it was no more than three per cent. European interest rates were in general higher than this.

Just why the difference in interest rates between Europe and the United States should be so marked is a difficult question to answer fully. But at the risk of oversimplification it might be said that at least in the late 1950s the European governments faced problems of inflation and thus high interest rates were needed, whereas the American Government never achieved the same high level of employment and did not in general have to rely on high interest rates to stave off an inflation crisis. Indeed low interest rates were widely used to stimulate industrial growth in the American economy.

In 1957 and 1958 the discrepancy between British and American interest rates was particularly marked; the Bank of England introduced the seven per cent Bank Rate – unprecedented in the postwar period. Foreign holders of dollar assets who were in a position to do so found it convenient in some cases to bank with British or European banks and so obtain the higher interest rates.

Thus – somewhat obscurely, it must be admitted – the market grew. The European banks borrowed and lent dollars on a short-term basis, trusting in their ability to give higher interest rates to lenders and offer cheaper service charges to borrowers, to conduct business in dollars which might otherwise have passed through other hands.

The situation was at once a compliment and an embarrassment to the American monetary authorities. It increased the use of the dollar as an international currency, and so increased world liquidity. But since the market was largely outside the control of these authorities it was also a potential source of difficulty during a currency crisis.

The market is continually expanding and evolving. Even to put its characteristics down on paper is to run the risk of being outdated. But if its origins are obscure, its future is uncertain. All that can be done is to remark on some of the more recent developments in the situation. The Eurodollar market is dominated by the British banks, who appear to conduct about eighty per cent of the transactions in Europe. However, two widely differing groups appear to be entering the field. The first of these are the American commercial banks, who hope through branch offices in Europe to attract a share in the market: the second is the Russian banking system, which through its London branch appears also to be actively soliciting dollar accounts.

Apart from the Eurodollar market there are signs of Euro-sterling markets, and even of other currencies being operated in European centres, where similar conditions apply, but on a very much more limited scale.

Finally it may be added that the Eurodollar market seems to be spreading to the Middle East and beyond. While such developments must receive a mixed welcome from the American monetary authorities they represent at least a partial answer to the problem of increasing international liquidity; although with the apparent move from very short-term dollar loans to loans of two or more years, this aspect of the market may not be as important as is sometimes assumed.

Chapter 6

TRADE AND TARIFFS

BRITAIN'S economic prosperity, indeed her very existence, depends upon foreign trade; more than any other major nation, she has a vital interest in encouraging free trade.

The implications of this have appeared in the friction which has from time to time arisen between Britain and her American ally on trade with Communist territories, and in the efforts of British governments to secure fairly free trade throughout the world, regardless of the political complexions of the customers. It must be said, however, that British interests in freer trade have from time to time conflicted with sectional interests at home, and with political aims abroad, such as Commonwealth unity, and it is doubtful whether it is going to be easier in the future to reconcile conflicting interests than it is proving today.

The case for free trade

The case for free trade between nations is in theory unanswerable; nevertheless no country nowadays wholeheartedly subscribes to it.

Britain's prosperity in the nineteenth century was built on free trade, and the British Government and all the economists of the day endorsed the system enthusiastically. Nevertheless the merits of free trade were not so obvious to many of the nations which were themselves attempting to follow Britain's lead into industrialization. For it was plainly difficult for any newly established and therefore as yet relatively inefficient industry in, for example, the United States to compete successfully, even on its home market, with the long established British industry enjoying all the advantages of established expertise and a mass market. To prevent such infant industries being killed off by premature exposure to the harsh winds of competition, the Americans and many other countries imposed tariffs against British imports, which as well as bringing in revenue protected the home industries and gave them a chance to grow in a protected home market.

To the British of course such action seemed folly, in that it raised the costs to the Americans themselves. But after a generation, the American industries had not just survived but had grown to the point where they could challenge the older British industries, not only on the American market, which was still protected, but also in other areas, even in the British home market; it now began to seem that there was a good deal of method in the folly.

Was the world as a whole better off because America, Germany and others were now challenging British industrial supremacy? Possibly not, if one argues that large-scale production for a world market would have made British goods even cheaper. But the Americans and the Germans were better off, even if the world over-all economic position was worsened.

It is this fact which makes nonsense of many of the economic arguments against tariffs. It may be true to say that tariffs leave the world as a whole worse off; but they may leave the individual countries which impose the tariffs much better off.

The arguments for tariffs have been reinforced by the experience of the 1930s, which showed how rapidly depression can spread from one country to another. Tariffs may be mutually self-defeating, but as a means of containing newly regained prosperity a tariff may help individual nations to climb out of depressions, albeit at the expense of treading on other nations in the process.

Quite apart from the economic arguments which may encourage a government to adopt tariffs, there may be non-economic arguments which are at least as valid. The protection of an industry which is regarded as vital to defence, or of a way of life which is regarded as socially worth maintaining, are obvious examples. The protection which most countries afford to agriculture is possibly the most widespread of these basically non-economic motives.

The British record so far as tariffs are concerned has been

chequered. The nineteenth century was the heyday of the doctrine of free trade and Britain was its leading advocate. There were few customs duties and in most cases these were balanced by an equivalent excise duty on home-produced goods of the same type.

The move away from free trade began in the First World War with tariffs against inessential imports; like many other wartime expedients, these were continued in peacetime, mainly in the case of industries whose retention on military grounds was felt to be essential. At this time began the practice of discriminatory tariffs, whereby Commonwealth imports were subject to a lower tariff than imports from elsewhere – the beginning of the Imperial Preference system.

The end of the gold standard in 1931 marked a move towards general protection. It was in many ways a retrograde step, but in a world of 'beggar my neighbour' policies, with every nation liable to discriminate against imports to encourage home production and to foster exports as a means of exporting unemployment, it was perhaps inevitable. At the same time the principle of Imperial Preference* was systematized at the Ottawa Conference of 1932. The mutual arrangements among Commonwealth members to give preferential treatment to each other roused considerable resentment, especially in the United States. The concept was linked in the minds of Americans with the appearance of the Sterling Bloc about the same time, although in fact the two were not identical in area, and to a large extent this accounts for the hostility which the Americans expressed to the Sterling Area system in the last years of the war, when they seemed to be out to destroy it if they could.

British tariffs in the 1930s probably did afford a measure of help to home industry, and caused an increase in the level of employment in Britain, although the effect on world economic production was probably adverse. Similarly the Ottawa Agreements probably had the effect of increasing inter-Commonwealth trade, to the benefit of members, but they decreased total world trade rather more. In an era of mutual selfish national behaviour, Britain probably could not have done very much else than imitate

* See pp. 35–6.

the policies of her main competitors. Nevertheless it was a situation from which no major trading nation emerged with much credit, and it was the reaction to this which made for some of the idealism of the postwar planning which took place during the early war years.

The Americans, who had been among the worst offenders, became the greatest idealists, with a somewhat tiresome habit of lecturing other nations on evil practices from which they had not been entirely immune themselves. Idealism faded again and has to some extent been replaced by a hard-headed realization that, even on the most selfish of national motives, mutual forbearance on tariff restrictions and mutual bargaining is possibly the best solution to many international problems.

In the early enthusiasm and idealism of wartime the American Government had propounded the concept of an International Trade Organization to set up codes of behaviour in international trade. The proposal, which was met with some scepticism by those nations which had experience of American prewar policy, was nevertheless pressed with some vigour by the American Government, and was finally completed at a conference in Havana in 1948. It was envisaged as the third of the great postwar plans, along with the I.M.F. and the World Bank.

The International Trade Organization was conceived by the United States, and strangled at birth by the United States. Conscious of mounting hostility to the concepts of freer trade, which in the last resort were to attack American practices as much as those of any other power, the American administration decided not to submit it for Congressional ratification, and the product of four years' idealism and hard work disappeared.

The result of this abrupt change of policy was the emergence of what had hitherto been regarded as essentially a stop-gap measure, the General Agreement on Tariffs and Trade. G.A.T.T. assumed an importance which matched that of the defunct I.T.O., and in its more practical approach to the question of international trade made progress at a faster pace than might have seemed possible.

The General Agreement on Tariffs and Trade

The principle on which G.A.T.T. operates is a general application of the 'most-favoured-nation' clause. This clause, which grew in importance in the interwar period of trade restrictions, amounts to an undertaking given by one nation to another that any trade concession offered to a third nation in the future would automatically apply to it as well. This of course was a form of trade discrimination which positively invited trade restrictions as bargaining counters, since there was little chance of negotiating most-favoured-nation terms with a country unless there could be reciprocal concessions which had some meaning. In time the most-favoured-nation clause had become rather less effective once it was the rule rather than the exception.

G.A.T.T. followed this principle to its logical conclusion. Regular meetings were to be held at which all members would be able to make individual bargains for mutual tariff concessions with each other. Literally thousands of such mutual tariff reductions could be made at such conferences. Once such an agreement were made the concession in tariff rates would then become available to all members of G.A.T.T. on a most-favoured-nation clause principle.

The mutual tariff restrictions were not to be weakened by the simultaneous imposition of another form of restriction, such as quotas or licensing – forms of control which had grown up in the interwar years.

There were exceptions of course: any discriminatory arrangement which had existed before the creation of G.A.T.T. could be continued, although new ones could not be made. The most important pre-G.A.T.T. discriminatory system was probably Imperial Preference.

The success of G.A.T.T. has been heartening, especially since it was originally designed as a merely transient system to be replaced by the more ambitious I.T.O. The reductions were in general negotiated for a fixed period of three years, and in view of the mass bargaining procedures it was necessary to hold tariff-reducing conferences every few years. These have been held at

Geneva, Annecy and Torquay; it seems likely that Geneva meetings will become the rule rather than the exception.

Much of the early impetus has gone out of G.A.T.T. In a sense this is a tribute to its success in the early days, and to the fact that in many cases tariffs have been reduced to so low a level that there is little scope for further bargaining. In the main the emphasis in recent years has been on the elimination of other methods of restriction. These have been permitted only in respect of agricultural protection, which has always proved a problem in international trade; as a device to protect newly created and as yet uncompetitive industries; and finally to protect the balance of payments situation.

As has been mentioned, agriculture has always been regarded as an exception, and all countries tend to protect this section of the economy. While there is plenty of room for dispute on the terms of agricultural trade, no nation is really in any position to criticize the restrictive practices of any other in this field: it is highly unlikely that G.A.T.T. will ever remedy the situation.

As for the newly created industry, there is an argument for protecting it in its early stages when it is not likely to be competitive against imports from long-established industries overseas. This argument would seem particularly valid for a newly developing country which hopes to industrialize. Indeed the whole field of special treatment for these developing countries is one where G.A.T.T. might be able to establish some general principles.

The main type of non-tariff restriction which has been employed in the postwar world is of course the use of monetary controls. There is no real difference between forbidding the import, say, of an American motor car by imposing a very high tariff, and the practice of allowing its import but refusing the supplier the right to convert his local currency earnings back into dollars. Two types of monetary control were prevalent in the early postwar years: the blocked-currency system, whereby currency earned by the sale within a country of goods which were regarded as non-essentials could not be converted; and the multiple exchange rate system, whereby the exchange rate offered depended on the type of goods which were being sold.

186

With the increase of convertibility, these practices, which were justified on the grounds of an adverse balance of payments situation, have largely disappeared. But it is as well to remember that, while the pace of tariff reductions achieved through G.A.T.T. has slowed down in the 1960s, it is probable that these reductions may be rather more genuine than sweeping cuts in the past which were stultified by the use of non-tariff methods of discrimination.

The attitude of G.A.T.T. to arrangements for integration among countries is of crucial importance. Briefly it may be said that customs unions are considered acceptable under G.A.T.T. rules, although in a sense a customs union does represent discrimination against outside nations. A customs union is created when two or more nations agree to have completely free trade between each other and to operate a common tariff against outside countries. The Benelux Union of Belgium, the Netherlands and Luxemburg is an example of a customs union; and the Common Market, once its timetable is complete, internal tariffs have disappeared and all members have the same external tariff, will also be a customs union. In a sense too the fifty States of the United States, having freedom of commerce, represent a customs union that is also a political union.

G.A.T.T. recognizes and approves of customs unions on the ground that they will increase freedom of international trade between the countries, while the common external tariff, based presumably on some average of the tariffs of the individual countries, will not increase discrimination. Customs unions are likely to increase in importance, and preliminary attempts have been made to establish them in Africa, the Middle East and South America, in imitation of the Common Market. Whether they will succeed is as yet problematic.

While G.A.T.T. approves of customs unions and so of the Common Market, its attitude towards a free trade area system of varying external tariffs is more equivocal. A common tariff or a customs union can be accepted as averaging out individual tariffs and therefore seems unobjectionable. A free trade area with varying tariffs creates in one sense yet another discriminatory system. Certainly the European Free Trade Association has had rather more difficulty than the Common Market in reconciling its policies with that of G.A.T.T.

The Kennedy Round

In the past America's record on tariff reductions has not been particularly good. The massive industrialization of the United States was achieved behind tariff walls and even when America's competitive position was clearly established tariffs continued to be the rule rather than the exception. Many American industrialists wanted to reduce tariffs in return for similar concessions for their exports, but the bargaining position of the American Government was very much hampered by the extremely burdensome separation-of-powers doctrine – which went a long way to ensure that, whatever the President might from time to time want in the way of tariff reductions, there was nothing to prevent Congress from pursuing a quite different course. The political system of the United States puts a premium, moreover, on the individual members of the House of Representatives following purely parochial interests in protecting industries in their own districts. The result has been that sectional interests have been often put ahead of national interests, and no President has ever been quite sure that any arrangements made by the Executive would be accepted by the Legislature (i.e. Congress).

What a tariff negotiator needs is the power to make concession for concession: in the past this has been rather difficult to attain. But by the early 1960s the United States accepted this principle; and during the 'Dillon Round', largely on American initiative, cuts of about twenty per cent were achieved on over 4,000 items between 1961 and 1962. The creation of the Common Market played an important role in ensuring American interest, for the U.S., with agricultural exports of over $1,000 million annually, has a considerable stake in the European market.

The U.S. Trade Expansion Act of 1962 gave the President unprecedented powers to bargain with other countries under the review which was due in 1963–4. In some instances the President was empowered to negotiate down to zero tariffs in 'across the board' negotiations. These powers, however, were based on the expectation of a successful British application for Common Market membership, and with the failure of those negotiations much of the powers became pointless.

What remained, however, was the 'Kennedy Round', the authority for the President to negotiate a fifty per cent cut in all tariffs, with minimal exceptions.

The American Government has a particular interest in safeguarding its agricultural exports to the Common Market, and would presumably be willing to trade concessions in industrial products, such as motor cars, for such safeguards. This brings American interests very much into conflict with French. The French economy has undergone a dramatic revolution in recent years, not least in agriculture, and so far as France is concerned therefore the Common Market is a large market for this French surplus. German agriculture is, by this standard, not particularly advanced and enjoys a fair measure of protection still, in spite of French efforts to penetrate this market. There is no doubt that the Germans would be willing to offer agricultural tariff concessions to the Americans, provided that some protection could be afforded to German home producers. Tactically it would be easier to ensure this protection against American imports than against imports from a fellow-member of E.E.C. The conflict of interest this represents does not augur well either for the development of the European Economic Community or for the success of current tariff negotiations.

Tariff disparities

With the Trade Expansion Act the American authorities had come far from their previous stance of high tariffs, and 'Buy American' policies. Unfortunately, but all too humanly perhaps, the more liberal American approach was being formulated at the very time when French, and ultimately Common Market, attitudes were beginning to harden. The American authorities envisaged reciprocal tariff cuts of fifty per cent by member nations, with only a few exceptions. In this approach they were supported by the British, who saw in a drastic lowering of tariffs a means of moderating the inevitable ill-effects of the failure of their Common Market negotiations.

As it happened, in many of the instances where tariffs could be reduced, the American tariffs were very high compared with the equivalent European tariffs in whose lowering the Americans were interested. Prompted by the French, the Common Market authorities argued that where these disparities in tariff levels existed, an over-all fifty per cent cut would mean much more benefit to the Americans than to the Common Market countries.

The Common Market formula for dealing with such a one-sided bargain would involve the imposition of different reductions where the disparity between the duty in the low tariff of one country and in the high tariff elsewhere amounts to one half or less. The proposals were that the lower-tariff country would be required to offer only a twenty-five per cent cut to the other country's fifty per cent.

While there is a certain equity about such an arrangement, a complication immediately arises over third parties, since any G.A.T.T. arrangement must be applied to all members. It might, for example, happen that the Common Market countries wished to invoke the disparity procedure in respect of a commodity which they import partly from the United States but in the main from a third country, perhaps a Free Trade Association member. The main loser from the disparity arrangements would then be not the United States, whose tariff provoked the use of the disparity procedure, but the main suppliers, whose tariff policy might have been a good deal more liberal than the Americans'. The implications of this aroused resistance to the procedure by such countries as Britain, which no doubt, in the process of resisting, further acquired the odium of representing American interests in Europe.

Mutual compromise only just saved the negotiations. But the rising sense of independence from the United States, of which the disparities dispute is but one instance among many, and the replacement of idealism by national calculation within the

Common Market have probably gone far to ensure that there will be no dramatic breakthrough in Atlantic trade. The *élan* has gone, from the European movement, from the Atlantic movement, and with it the prospects of a rapid advance from the Kennedy Round. In the late 1960s there is a danger that, following a decade of advance, the liberal movement in international economic affairs is beginning to slow down.

Tariffs and other constraints on trade: their effect on location of industries

Tariffs, and for that matter currency restrictions, can have a marked effect in not merely restraining trade, but in reallocating entire industries. The point can be illustrated by the creation of the Australian car industry, or the creation of several new industries in Britain since the war.

Australia like most countries would like to have a national car industry. For a relatively small population, skilled, but not so highly skilled as to earn a reputation for quality engineering superior to that, say, of Britain or the Continental car manufacturers, the prospects of competing successfully with those manufacturers who had been established for many years and enjoyed a secure mass market at home were not very great.

The Australian Government imposed a tariff directed primarily against the main suppliers, the U.S. and British car industries. It would have been possible for them to accept the loss of sales, and the Australian public might have been reconciled to paying a higher price for imported cars. But a tariff such as this can make it cheaper to import car components rather than the finished car. The labour costs of assembly are not then subject to the tariff.

The first step is thus an assembly plant, with all components imported. Gradually, however, it becomes possible to manufacture some of the components locally, so that the total tariff burden is reduced to the specifically imported components only. Since the average car manufacturer in America or Britain is operating an assembly plant putting together subcontracted components in many cases, the transition from an Australian assembly plant to an Australian car-producing factory is not very great. It is possible then to foresee that virtually all the components will in time be manufactured locally. The only qualification of course is that the product is being produced to the specifications of the original British or American car. A specifically designed car can only be achieved when everything is being produced locally – and it may be that die castings and so on are imported from the parent company. In this way a small but thriving Australian car industry has been created, based in the first instance on U.S. motor subsidiaries and more recently on British ones too. Much the same process has led to the assembly of Continental cars in the United Kingdom, or the Italian Fiat as the Spanish Seat.

These cases illustrate how tariffs and quota restrictions can be used to create industries in places where they might otherwise be disinclined to go. Indeed it may well happen that such a subsidiary company in time loses its connexion with the parent company. It may require further capitalization, taken up by shareholders in the country where the subsidiary is situated. Fords of Great Britain for example had until recently only a minority share interest held by the parent company, which had eventually to make a take-over bid for complete control.

A second possibility is that the subsidiary company may eventually replace the parent company. Examples are to be found in Britain. A number of American firms facing a mixed bag of problems – high labour costs at home, tariffs and currency controls – set up British factories shortly after the war, initially to serve the British market. Within a few years, however, some of them have been invading the American home market. At least one American company, Burroughs, has finally closed down the parent company, and used its British and Continental companies to serve the American market as well.

Some of the pressure towards this process has gone, since monetary restrictions have been eased in the 1950s and 1960s. Nevertheless the existence of tariff barriers, behind which lie rich potential markets, has done a good deal to ensure that a relatively new type of foreign trade has developed in recent years – the export of industries, rather than of commodities. National companies may become international corporations, or even indeed simply change their nationality and place of residence.

The creation of the Common Market has spurred on American investment inside the new tariff walls, to the delight of some, and the chagrin of others. The possibility of a split in Europe between the Free Trade Association countries and the Common Market countries is very real. But some of the more disastrous consequences have been mitigated by the readiness of large companies to set up or buy up subsidiaries on the other side of the tariff walls.

It is to be hoped that the tariff walls go down instead of up. But whether they do or not, we are likely to see more and more Continental cars on British roads and British cars on the Continent. The only point of difference will be whether foreign-designed cars have been assembled, or even manufactured, more efficiently in the parent factories, or rather less so in local subsidiaries.

Chapter 7

THE DEVELOPING NATIONS

THE situation of the 'have nots' of this world, the poorer 'developing' nations, has been described as a time bomb ticking away the hours. It is potentially the most dangerous political situation in the world today, for its undertones go beyond the ideologies of capitalism and Communism to the more sinister emotions of race.

The problem has been very crudely aligned with the Cold War, and it has been argued that if the West will not help the Communists will take over. While this remains an ever-present possibility, the actual situation may be more complex, for with the growing affluence of the Russian Communist Bloc arises the possibility that the split will be on racial rather than political lines.

The situation is dangerous, but it is by no means hopeless, for the conscience of the richer nations has been stirred uncomfortably. What is needed is not just aid – although plenty of that is required – so much as a conscious effort to wipe out the built-in bias which modern technology has created against many of the developing nations.

Britain's role in this situation is bound to be rather marginal. British contributions amount to about eight per cent of the total Western aid, and with minor exceptions have been confined to the Commonwealth. Nevertheless an intelligent lead by Britain in encouraging freer and more equitable trade between the rich nations and the poor might give her an influence out of all proportion to her size in solving this problem.

The developing countries

At least one third of the world is hungry. This is one of the stark facts of the modern world – a fact that overshadows political problems. The situation of the hungry third is not improving much: in fact there is plenty of evidence that it is worsening.

As industrial countries grow richer, and the conditions of life there improve dramatically, as large sections of Western Europe and North America move towards what has become loosely characterized as the affluent society, huge areas of the world grow hungrier. As the rich get richer, the poor get poorer. The answer to the problem of these hungry millions appears to be industrialization, and the underdeveloped countries strive blindly towards the Western means of production, Western goals, and above all a Western standard of living. In this chapter we shall be discussing these underdeveloped areas and the role of Britain in alleviating some of the misery of their struggles.

There have been in the past, and there are yet today, some serious misconceptions of what is meant by an underdeveloped nation, and it is useful to attempt to define what exactly the problems of development are.

Part of the trouble might well be a mistaken sense of international tact. Even the term 'underdeveloped nations' is being replaced by another phrase 'the emerging nations', on the ground, one supposes, that the former term has semantic undertones of inferiority. Unfortunately it is the use of such tactful terms which can lead to confusion. An underdeveloped nation is presumably one which is short of capital and able to absorb it and put it to the best possible use. Such a nation then is one which can use more capital and presumably, since there is an acute shortage, there will be a high return on its use. If this is the definition, then Canada, Australia, and even the United States are underdeveloped nations.

This is not quite what people normally mean by an underdeveloped nation, which is, if one might put it crudely, one with a backward economy, which is able to provide its citizens with only a miserably low standard of living. Its backwardness may be due to overpopulation, primitive agricultural and industrial methods, lack of resources, illiteracy, hunger, disease, a hopelessly backward system of government, or any combination of these factors. But to lump such countries as 'underdeveloped', in the way that Australia, Canada and the United States are underdeveloped, is a mistaken kindness, for the problems of a backward country are far different.

The confusion of terms has led to trouble, and still leads to trouble. At the risk again of oversimplification, the fact that a backward economy desperately needs help to modernize itself and therefore suffers from a grave shortage of capital does not mean that it can readily attract capital or, even if it does, absorb it successfully.

An illustration can be readily derived from the experience of India. In 1947 India was the underdeveloped nation *par excellence*. Newly independent, with a vast population and a tremendous need for capital for investment and industrialization, it seemed to represent the ideal area for heavy overseas investment. So perturbed was the Indian Government over the possibility that this massive investment would bring foreign domination that it passed legislation to prevent an undue element of foreign control over the vital sectors of the economy. The Indians, in short, feared foreign economic exploitation. One of the more humiliating discoveries for the Indian Government has been the conspicuous lack of enthusiasm among foreign investors to move in. The Indian economy desperately lacked capital, but in the judgement of private foreign investors this shortage of capital was not matched by an ability to absorb it on conditions which would give a reasonable return to the investor. Although India is more desperately short of capital than America, an investment in the former is less likely to yield a respectable return than an investment in the latter.

This confusion between the need for capital for industrialization and the ability to absorb it usefully is one of those characteristics which have been misinterpreted in the past. The role of private investment overseas can be very much overemphasized, for the returns are likely to be small, and the risks great.

This is not, of course, to say that there will be no overseas private investment. The massive British investment throughout the world in the nineteenth century demonstrated that the private investor could play an important part in the transformation of a developing nation. But, whether in Africa, Asia or South America, the types of industry which attracted overseas investment from Britain or Europe were remarkably similar. Indeed investment was fairly closely confined to a small sector of the economy; and the criteria which applied to private investment in the nineteenth century still apply today.

Extractive industries

What type of private industry will attract overseas investment in an underdeveloped country? Not in all likelihood a consumer-goods industry supplying the nation itself, since the home market is likely to prove exceedingly poor. Instead the industry most likely to be of interest to the foreign investor is one which serves a foreign market in a developed country. This in practice means some form of extractive industry, an oil well, mine, or a planta-tion producing raw materials for industrial markets elsewhere.

Thus the aim of the foreign investor is firstly to create the extractive industry, and then to get the raw materials out of the country in the shortest possible time. The effects of this new industry in the underdeveloped country are therefore minimal.

The reasons for the policy are obvious. Any processing of materials is likely to be better carried on in an industrial country. In addition there is at least a tacit recognition that the more the manufacturing process can be kept outside the control of the underdeveloped country the less vulnerable the investor will be to the vagaries of political unrest and possible confiscation.

The point is well illustrated by the crisis which followed the Persian Government's nationalization of the Anglo-Iranian Oil Company in 1951. The nationalization of oil wells by themselves would have been of little consequence, since without the means of refining and selling the crude oil the expropriator was likely to lose more than the expropriated, who might have alternative supplies. The difficulty in 1951 was that the Company had just completed a massive refinery at Abadan and this was also seized. The decision to build this must have been bitterly regretted by the Company for it made the task of bringing the Persian Govern-ment into a more reasonable frame of mind that much more difficult. A combination of factors eventually brought about a compromise solution: these included the legal tactics of the

Anglo-Iranian Company, who challenged the sales of oil made by the Iranian authorities after the take-over, making foreign buyers reluctant to buy it, and the overthrow of the nationalizing Mossadeq régime in Iran. But, as a study of the factors which make it possible for a foreign company to fight expropriation by denying access to vital processes, the whole story is difficult to parallel. At the end of it all no one had won decisively. The Anglo-Iranian Oil Company had been replaced by a consortium, and the large market which Persian oil had enjoyed had gone for at least a decade, being rapidly replaced by alternative sources of supply. But the lesson has not been lost on oil companies or the producer nations; and the fact that the oil revenues of the producers have increased, while even in the midst of anti-Western crises there have been few attempts to repeat the nationalization tactics of the Persian Government, illustrates their interdependence.

But if it is in the interests of the foreign investor that the extractive industry, and only the extractive industry, should be sited in the producing country, the interests of the latter depend on having as much as possible of the industry from raw-material extraction to finished processing carried on in the country. This is, of course, not merely for the political advantage of having an integrated industry completely within the country, but, even more important, because of the problem of achieving balanced growth.

Some raw-material producers with the highest per capita incomes are also the most primitive of societies. An Arab oil producer may have oil wells, pipelines and an ocean terminal. Beyond this, nothing. To what extent is the enormous oil revenue which may accrue, and possibly be misspent by the ruler, aiding the country? The truth may be that the extractive industry contributes literally nothing but revenues to the economy, which may be completely primitive.

If, however, the terminal is equipped with a refinery, and the tankers load not crude oil, but refined products, the beginnings of industrialization have been made. In all likelihood the key jobs will be held by foreign specialists. But the employment of any type of native labour means an increase in skills, and almost inevitably the proportion of skilled native labour will grow through the years. The process may be speeded by laws attempting to regulate the proportion of foreign personnel which may be employed.

The attitude of the owners of the foreign firm towards this policy may vary from enthusiastic cooperation to outright hostility, depending perhaps on how they foresee the probable course of events. If they anticipate a stable government in their host country they may well be content to push a policy of training local personnel to the limit: if they fear expropriation they will naturally hesitate to offer hostages to fortune in the shape, not merely of a viable industrial unit, but – even more important – of competent local staff. Unfortunately, of course, mistrust breeds mistrust, and there is no easy escape from the spiral thus set up.

It is not perhaps without significance that after the salutary lessons of the Iranian seizures oil companies are now among the most progressive in training local staff, having demonstrated to the oil-producing nations their comparative independence of any one country's supplies.

We have seen, then, that it will be in the interest of the foreign investor to invest primarily in extractive industries: perhaps logically this leads into the industries directly related to these – to transport and public utilities. At one time or another probably most of the mines, oil wells and railways of Africa, Asia and Latin America were owned by American, British or Continental-based companies. Nationalism plus perhaps a dwindling record of profitability have led to the gradual nationalization of these assets. Nevertheless they do represent at least the first wave of foreign investment in an underdeveloped country – and of them all perhaps only the railways and utilities make a substantial contribution towards the industrialization of that country: purely extractive industries clearly do not, unless the investor can be prevailed upon to set up processing industries as well – and often he cannot be so persuaded.

The alternative to private investment

So far we have seen that it cannot be taken for granted that private investment will go where it is most urgently needed, and that even where private investment makes economic sense there may be very potent political factors working against it. In the second half of the twentieth century private investment overseas is likely to be quite insufficient for the needs of the developing world.

If private investment is both inadequate and risky, there remains the possibility of massive loans or grants by governments which on political or simply moral grounds wish to see the hungry of the world prosper, or at least avoid starvation. Since the war there has been a dramatic upsurge of such loans or grants – and the results have been quite inadequate to the resources offered.

Sometimes the aid is directed to the wrong ends. Some industries carry prestige, others do not. It will often be the case that ostentatious capital projects – building a steel plant where there is no sustained demand for its products, or a dam where there is inadequate potential for the hydroelectric power – appeal to a newly independent nation rather more than a more mundane and practical industry, like textiles, which is immediately required. Vast quantities of precious capital can be squandered on items which are essentially prestige-bearing, and any outsider criticizing such ostentatious behaviour is liable to be not merely disregarded, but resented.

There is in this national context a 'demonstration' effect, whereby nations as well as individuals seek the symbols of industrial progress long before they have achieved the realities of this development.

What is required is of course balanced growth rather than prestige growth – but politically this is not very attractive because it is not very spectacular. In some respects of course prestige growth appears to be a saving of scarce resources. Why spend scarce capital on what could be classified as unessentials?

The answer to this lies in the tremendous implications of

poverty, and of inflation, in an underdeveloped country. If one might revert to scientific jargon, the marginal propensity to save in a poor country is very low. This simply means that a hungry man is more likely to spend any extra money he obtains on food than to save it.

If, when there is extra investment in a primitive economy, bringing extra jobs and extra wages, virtually none of this extra purchasing power is saved, then we have what amounts to an infinite chain reaction. The new wages mean an increased demand for food: the increased income to the food producers means an increased demand by them for some commodity: and the increased wages for the producers of this commodity mean increased demand for, and wages in, another section of the economy: and so on, *ad infinitum*. This chain reaction is not appreciably diminished as long as each new recipient of income in turn spends all, rather than saves: and in practice the economy does not respond rapidly to the increased demand by increased production. There is the same amount of food, the same amount of commodities. All the situation is likely to produce is a rampant inflation. It is entirely justified to envisage a situation where £1 million of extra jobs could create £100 million of extra demand without a single new item being produced by the economy to meet the new demand, because the economy is simply not geared to produce above the normal demand.

In a situation like this, all that the new investment, which was intended to help produce a Westernized industrial economy, has achieved is to destroy the old but viable system without replacing it, and the economic and political consequences are incalculable.

The poorer the country is at the beginning of the process, the more exaggerated the inflationary consequences may be. Is there an alternative, or is inflation inevitable? There are in fact several alternatives but none of them is particularly palatable.

The answer to the problem of the chain reaction is to absorb the increased purchasing power. In a wealthy economy this could be achieved tolerably well by private savings, but, as we have seen, in a primitive and hungry community this is just not possible.

The most popular method is of course to supply more food and more commodities than the old economy can produce, i.e. by importing more to meet increased demand. As a means of averting inflation an import surplus is exceedingly efficacious. But it merely substitutes a balance of payments crisis for an inflationary crisis. In some respects a balance of payments crisis is a status symbol for any self-respecting underdeveloped country.

A second alternative is to replace the non-existent savings by forced savings, namely by imposing such a rate of taxation that the extra purchasing power of the new wages simply does not exist. There are several obvious disadvantages. For such a measure to be fully effective, the employees would have to be left as poor as ever. In such a situation clearly there would be little incentive for them to seek new work in the new industries. A further problem is that the government machinery of the old system would almost certainly be quite ill-prepared on the technical side to operate at such a level of efficiency as to deprive the wage-earners of all the benefits.

This then is the dilemma which may face the underdeveloped country seeking to industrialize and so raise its standards of living. It is not only short of capital, but, if it is given or lent the wherewithal from overseas to develop its resources, it may find that its economy is unable readily to absorb the new purchasing power created without runaway inflation on the one hand, or a serious balance of payments problem on the other. Faced with the vast problems thus raised, it is understandable, if highly regrettable, that many of the governments concerned have abandoned their pretensions to democracy and persuasion, and resorted to the totalitarianism of forced labour to solve their economic problems.

What can be done by the Western democracies to aid these countries? Clearly the level and type of aid could be stepped up – not merely the obvious type of aid, the capital equipment, etc., but even possibly some less obvious commodities, indeed luxuries, if only to absorb the excess purchasing power which is created.

Over-population and under-employment

One of the most depressing aspects of an underdeveloped country is that it is frequently over-populated with respect to its resources.

Over-population, it may be remarked, is a relative term. Few of the underdeveloped countries have a density of population even approaching that of the United Kingdom. It is a matter of dispute whether Britain is over-populated; it would be ridiculous to argue that it was disastrously over-populated. Clearly a definition of over-population makes sense only if it is related to the production of the economy. Most of the so-called over-populated regions have the vast majority of their population engaged in producing the merest necessities of life. The United Kingdom, with only a tiny fraction of its manpower engaged in food production, is scarcely overcrowded by this criterion. Were the majority of British workers forced to grow food the situation would be vastly different.

Over-population is unnatural – an unnatural result of human progress. Left to herself nature has her own grim methods of keeping the balance of population and food. But what happened to Britain in the eighteenth century is happening on an immensely vaster scale in Africa, Asia and Latin America today – the staggering rise in population, resulting not from an increase in the birth rate, but rather a drastic fall in the death rate. The traditional enemy, disease, is being beaten by medical science; but those who are escaping from their traditional enemy are facing a more insidious one, malnutrition, and the most deadly of all, starvation. As the populations grow exponentially, the problem of feeding them becomes more and more acute.

During the Industrial Revolution Britain solved the problem by a technological breakthrough in food production, and as a result, in the vital race between increased production and increased population, production won. That the result will be the same throughout the world in the twentieth century is by no means certain. If the population of a country increases by four per cent per annum and national production increases by three per cent the results will be inexorable. Sooner or later the population will be adjusted to an equilibrium by starvation.

This is precisely the problem that faces many of these nations, that production, and especially food production, increases less rapidly than population: the standard of living falls towards starvation level and the limits this imposes. As the industrial nations of the world increase in wealth, the gap between their affluence and the despair of the underdeveloped poses an acute moral and political problem which will be with us for the rest of the century.

Allied to the harsh realities of over-population is the less obvious but no less significant problem of under-employment. It is one of the ironies of politics that family affection – or rather interdependence – seems to decline with progress. The family – or its extension, the tribe – may be the chief economic unit in a backward society. In a land-hungry society the younger members are not turned off to fend for themselves – a harsh process which nevertheless saw the younger son as the creator of so much industry and commerce in Britain when she faced the same problem. Indeed to parents facing old age with no state aid, a large and united family provides their only future. Thus the land which might support in comfort a small family has to support a large one, and the only hope of cultivating enough for all lies in the most intensive and backbreaking human toil by all, on very much diminishing returns. There is little real unemployment in the Western sense. But the heart-breaking human labour in tasks which could be more profitably done with a fraction of the human suffering, were capital to be employed properly, represents under-employment by any measure, because it is basically inefficient.

The fact of under-employment suggests, at least in theory, that it might be possible to obtain the extra labour to develop the industrial processes without seriously endangering the food supply if a means could be found of extricating some of the surplus workers from the land without increasing their total income. But the fatally easy method of achieving this object might be totalitarianism and forced labour – and the price exacted in forced labour and human misery has in the past proved to be very high.

How can the advanced nations help? By capital equipment perhaps. But capital equipment is often designed for use where the distribution of factors of production is totally different. A bulldozer may do as much work as five hundred men. But if the price of a bulldozer would pay for a thousand spades, may not the latter be a cheaper solution for an industrially backward nation? If labour-saving equipment is supplied, how appropriate is it in an over-populated region? Possibly as much equipment has rusted unused as has ever been used in the past decade.

A real problem facing the industrial nations offering aid is hostility. It has tended to be assumed that aid buys friendship; the rivalry between East and West in offering aid has shown the importance attached to this assumption. Thousands of millions of dollars of aid have been poured into the underdeveloped countries by America and Russia. Thousands of scholarships have been made available to students from these countries. But it is doubtful whether any substantial political gains have been made by either side; the underdeveloped nations of the Afro-Asian world have learned to play one side off against the other, without feeling undue gratitude towards either.

In giving aid, common sense as well as charity is needed. When a few years ago it was presented as a defeat for the West that Egypt had been persuaded by the Russians to accept hundreds of millions of dollars of aid from them rather than from the West, the logic of the argument must have seemed a little esoteric. And it is frankly conjectural whether in the long run the Russians have gained very much. Indeed, as has been said before, there seems to be an urge to be offensive rather than grateful to the bene-factors, to prove that the privilege of offering aid carries no favours. In a sense only a strong nation can afford to give aid, for a strong nation can accept the ingratitude such aid incurs. A good deal of forbearance may yet have to be asked of the British taxpayer in the face of such reactions.

Using the United Nations

It has often been suggested that if aid to underdeveloped countries were to be channelled through a United Nations agency, many of the touchy problems of oversensitivity among these nations could be avoided. The success of the World Bank, a U.N. agency, is instanced in support of this view.

While there is clearly a case for more aid in this direction it would be a mistake to imagine that all the problems of national pride would disappear.

In the first instance it is fairly certain that the agency would be heavily weighted on the side of the 'have not' countries: any recommendations made by these countries would depend on the willingness of the 'have' countries to meet the bills, and the effect of what would appear to the developed nations as extravagance in claims, and to the developing nations as niggardliness on the part of the developed nations, could cause even more friction than the comparatively undirected aid on a national basis now given.

Even more important perhaps is the assumption sometimes made that the world is merely divided into 'have' and 'have not' nations. It is readily accepted that there exist differences of interests among the 'have' nations. There is even yet in many people's minds an uncritical assumption that the 'have nots' are a homogeneous group of nations with mutual interests. This is a caricature of the true situation. There have already occurred instances where African nations, for example, have expressed resentment at the proportion of Western aid which had been directed towards Asia; and short of an absolute cornucopia of aid, any United Nations agency attempting to assess national needs and distribute limited aid would face an insoluble problem of conflicting interests.

A somewhat similar problem arose in the late 1940s when American aid was being supplied to Europe. The solution to the problem of conflicting and potentially vast claims on American generosity was the creation of the O.E.E.C. (the Organization for European Economic Cooperation), which in effect provided a system whereby European countries had to hammer out a total claim for aid which was arrived at after a mutual examination by the countries concerned of each others' claims. This was a practical solution, for it was evident that there was no shortage of financial and technological experts who could critically assess each country's claims.

Such an organization of the developing nations would be an ideal solution to the conflict of interest; but as a practical proposition it does not seem likely to work. There is an acute shortage of precisely the experts and technocrats in the developing countries who would achieve this, and even if there were sufficient enterprise, the resolution of conflicting claims from seventy or eighty countries of all stages of development and scattered across the globe would be wellnigh impossible.

It is of course only too easy to pour cold water, as has been done here, on idealistic schemes involving a United Nations takeover of the problem of the developing nations. But this is a problem which has yet to be solved – for the present administrative and financial machinery is patently inadequate.

The World Bank

There is already one United Nations agency providing useful but unfortunately inadequate resources which may marginally help the underdeveloped countries. This is the World Bank, or, to give it its more formal title, the International Bank for Reconstruction and Development, set up at the Bretton Woods Conference in 1944. The Bank was the complement of the International Monetary Fund. It has been less spectacular, less used and possibly more successful.

The role of the World Bank is to provide long-term loans either to governments or to private businesses which are able to obtain a government guarantee. It finances particular projects, of whose financial soundness it has been convinced, at rates of interest which are realistic if not high, for specified periods. It is important to appreciate this concept of loans for specific objects – the Bank does not exist merely to make unspecified loans to nations in financial difficulties.

It may lend money from its own resources, or it may raise loans by borrowing in world money markets. The advantages of this system are twofold. It enables the borrower to accept finance from an international institution and not from a foreign investor, and so is free from the taint of foreign domination: at the same time it enables the investor to lend to an international organization whose probity is beyond question and which is safe from expropriation.

As well as lending money the Bank may guarantee loans, but this power has not been used to any great extent.

The World Bank has in addition to its financial powers a considerable amount of technical expertise, and will examine and comment on any capital plan it may be asked to finance. Its expertise alone renders it invaluable to the underdeveloped country with few native experts.

The finances of the Bank were originally fixed at $10 billion made up of subscriptions from member countries. Two per cent of the subscription was payable in gold, and eighteen per cent in the member's currency; the other eighty per cent functions mainly as a guarantee for the moneys borrowed on the world markets. It is this eighty per cent reserve which removes the risk of non-payment by expropriation to which a lender to an underdeveloped country is often subject. When in 1958 the I.M.F. quotas were raised by fifty per cent the quotas of the World Bank were doubled, although no new quantities were drawn in cash. The reserve was therefore raised from eighty to ninety per cent.

During its first few years the Bank was mainly concerned in financing postwar reconstruction. Britain's financial contribution to this was small – her economy was hardly in a fit state to aid others. Latterly the emphasis of the Bank's finance-raising has moved away from the almost total domination by the American money market, and loans have been raised extensively throughout most of the world, apart from the Iron Curtain countries.

Its projects have been outstandingly successful. It has given good advice through its technical experts without giving offence: it has lent money without at the same time asserting any claims to ownership of the project, and with no political advantage for whatever country from which the Bank borrowed to finance its loan; and it has never had any of its loans subsequently repudiated. For to renege on a loan from the World Bank would be to renege on a United Nations organization and would undoubtedly mean that the prospects of that nation's ever being able to raise money on a national basis on the world's money markets would be so remote as to be virtually impracticable. In this sense the World Bank is truly a lender of last resort.

The success of the World Bank has been to a large extent due to its relatively modest approach to problems. Its aid has been limited to financially viable projects; and this has in practice put certain limitations not only on the types of projects which could be financed, but even on the countries which are likely to be able to avail themselves of its services. In short a certain amount of economic and political sophistication is needed in a society before it can contemplate and justify the economic activities which would make a World Bank loan practical.

The weight of the World Bank's lending has changed. In its earlier years it was used fairly extensively by European nations to rebuild their economies. Indeed as late as the middle 1950s the idea was being mooted that, to permit a vast amount of British capital investment in spite of the inevitable balance-of-payments crisis which this would cause, Britain might find it possible to finance an extensive programme of building nuclear-reactor power stations by a World Bank loan in dollars. This would have been stretching the intention of the World Bank charter to the limit and, fortunately perhaps, the idea came to nothing. But the very notion illustrates the situation that the World Bank found itself better able to lend to the developed, than to the underdeveloped countries.

In recent years, however, the emphasis in World Bank loans has been among the underdeveloped nations, and in this respect the Bank is fulfilling its most useful function. But the requirement of financial viability perhaps prevents the most critical needs of the desperately poor and backward nations being fulfilled by loans in this way. The Bank is thus of limited use save to those nations which are at least partly on the way to the 'take-off' point.

Subsidiary organizations

Apart from the World Bank itself there are now two subsidiary organizations which exist to supplement its rather limited resources and its even more limited terms of reference.

The first of these is the International Finance Corporation, which came into operation in 1956 and has the same staff and general aims as the World Bank. It is designed to assist the growth of private enterprise in underdeveloped areas. The World Bank has, by its nature, lent mainly for government projects. An I.F.C. loan does not need the government guarantee that a World Bank has, and is therefore likely to be more risky; its terms of reference are wider than the Bank's.

Although of course it has not the same security as the World Bank, operating as it does under its aegis, the I.F.C. has been as safe from default as the World Bank. But it has not operated on a very extensive scale. In the underdeveloped countries there is frequently not the technical competence to operate a massive private enterprise project which would be viable enough to qualify for aid. Any such scheme, supported by the government concerned, would almost certainly obtain the government guarantee needed to make it eligible for a World Bank loan. But the very fact that a government guarantee was not available would itself be a somewhat suspicious circumstance that might cause the I.F.C. to hesitate before advancing any loan.

In the very recent past a second such institution has been created. This is the International Development Association which is specifically intended to help those less developed countries which might have difficulty in meeting the stringent conditions of a World Bank loan. It provides long-term loans at very low interest rates, and the conditions are less stringent than the World Bank's. It is in fact a device for channelling aid into underdeveloped regions, and its potential significance in this context is far greater than its actual performance thus far. The I.D.A. might in time be one of the instruments whereby aid to the underdeveloped nations could be offered on a massive scale through the U.N.

Stabilizing world prices

Underdeveloped countries, if they are indeed able to earn foreign currencies, almost invariably do so by the export of raw materials, be they minerals or crops. The difficulty about relying on such exports is of course the excessive fluctuations in price to which they are subject. The comparative inability of these commodity producers to vary output readily in response to changes in demand means that prices are liable to be very high one season and very low in the next. The vagaries of price fluctuations are worsened by the fact that many such economies are dependent on the export of only one product. The one-crop or one-commodity economy is vulnerable to every fluctuation in price.

In most advanced countries the fluctuations of agricultural production are ironed out by some form of government intervention, be it a subsidy, a support price, or some form of minimum reserve price for commodities. This is done because it has been found expedient to remove this element of uncertainty over the price which a farmer can expect to receive each season for his crop. In much the same way it has frequently been suggested that some form of commodity scheme or support price be used to give a measure of stability to the commodity market, and at the same time to give some sort of guarantee of a stable return to the producers.

Basically there are two types of scheme, the commodity buffer stock scheme itself, and the quota scheme, although in practice a number of variations have been used.

The commodity buffer stock system depends on some international authority buying and selling the commodity within a certain range of prices. If the world price falls to a certain minimum point then the authority will buy on the open market, and thus create a buffer stock which can be released at times of high prices. Above a certain price the authority will sell from its stock.

There are of course a number of disadvantages. The principle cannot readily be applied to perishable commodities, or to any raw material, such as oil, which is comparatively expensive to store. Most metals, however, would create no particular problem.

The practical difficulties of the buffer system are great. Who constitutes the international authority and above all who finances the system? Clearly the ideal solution would be some form of council appointed by the leading producers and consumers, and financed by both. But in so far as the raw-material consumers are generally industrial countries enjoying a high standard of living, and the producers may be relatively poor, and so unable to put up much of the cost of the buffer stock, the scales tend to be weighted rather heavily in favour of the former. The countries who put up the finance are likely to have most say in fixing the minimum and maximum prices at which the council will buy and sell, and they will have an interest in keeping both prices as low as possible, while the producers will naturally favour the reverse.

Quite apart from the conflict of interests, it is really an extraordinarily difficult task to calculate the 'normal' price for a commodity, which would presumably be the half-way mark between the two prices. A wrong calculation could mean either that the buffer stock grew at a rapid pace until the fund on which it operated was exhausted – and the buffer might even contain several years' supply of the commodity: or at the other end it would simply not appear in the market at all since the price would never be low enough for it to buy. It is essential that a buffer stock must be regularly built up and regularly cleared if it is to be of any practical importance.

An unfortunate characteristic of raw-material producers is their tendency to over-produce in response to high prices, while failing to reduce output at a time of low prices. Although the buffer stock system may minimize the fluctuation of prices, it is liable at the same time to encourage the over-production by giving a secured market at a minimum price. Ultimately of course this tendency is likely to end with the exhaustion of the funds on which the buffer stock depends. The system might then break down having achieved nothing but the accumulation of perhaps several years' excessive supply.

There is another type of buffer stock, which has achieved some prominence in the postwar world. This has been the strategic stockpile. Shortages of vital raw materials had been an acute problem in the Second World War, and many countries, principally the United States, stockpiled quantities of strategic materials.

Unfortunately, however, as a means of moderating extreme variations in price the creation of strategic stockpiles is likely to do more harm than good. The strategic stockpiles have tended to be built up during times of international tension when raw-material prices have generally risen in any event. Thus the stockpile merely exaggerates the rise in prices. If the stockpiles are released again during a relaxation of international tension, then they may worsen a slump in prices. This is not of course an inevitable result, but it does illustrate the point that the effect of the creation of buffer stocks on prices depends very much on the motivation.

The alternative to the buffer stock is the quota system. This depends on the principle of restricting output when prices begin to fall, and sharing the market among the producers.

The advantage of the system is that it requires comparatively little financing; provided that agreement is reached among the nations on the size of the quotas, then there is no need to finance the scheme on any elaborate scale. Some of the methods of restricting output, such as the burning of coffee or wheat crops in the interwar years, have aroused considerable criticism, but in the case of minerals restrictions of output can be achieved by less spectacularly anti-social means.

There are a number of practical difficulties, however, in the concept of the quota. The most acute of these is the allocation of quotas between the producing nations. The most obvious basis of such quotas is a historical one, based on giving each nation a share depending on its production during a number of years. Unfortunately this system merely tends to perpetuate the advantage of the long-standing producers to the disadvantage of the new producers. While this does not exactly put a premium on inefficiency, it certainly does nothing to encourage improvements in techniques.

The system therefore has little to commend it to the more technically advanced producers, and perpetuates the declining producers where otherwise they would be driven from the market.

A further very practical difficulty is that there must be total cooperation by all producers in any quota system. A successful quota system which raises the price by depressing supplies presents a very great temptation to any producer to break the agreement, or to sanction unofficial excess marketing, since there can be little effective control of supplies.

The prewar attempts to restrict supplies of rubber appearing on world markets were limited in effect for this very reason. Malaya and Brazil, the chief producers, cooperated, but planters in the then Dutch East Indies, now Indonesia, did not.

As might be expected, of course, most commodity-price stabilization schemes are not clearly of the buffer stock or quota system, but a mixture of the elements of both.

The variety of the schemes is vast, but at the risk of sounding somewhat cynical it may be said that their common characteristic is that their success is at most limited. Where they have achieved some measure of success – the International Wheat Agreement being perhaps one instance – is where consumer and producer are of approximately the same economic strength. More typically, however, economically weak producer nations have been dealing with economically stronger consumer nations; and in general the weaker have gone to the wall. Possibly the first serious attempt to deal on a global scale with the problem has been the U.N. Conference on Trade and Development.

U.N.T.A.D. – the United Nations Conference on Trade and Development

The United Nations Conference on Trade and Development held at Geneva in the spring and summer of 1964 represented one of the most challenging attempts to confront the developed nations with their responsibilities to the developing. The driving force behind it was Dr Raul Prebisch, an Argentinian and the Secretary-General of the Conference. His thesis is possibly the best, and certainly one of the most moderate, expositions of the case for the developing nations, and it is worth looking at it in some detail – for it represents a situation which has been developing throughout the twentieth century and which may be the dominant political and economic factor of the last third of the century.

Dr Prebisch's thesis is simply that the comfortable nineteenth-century doctrine that international trade benefits all, and that the freer this trade can be made the greater will be the mutual benefits, was not only irrelevant, it was inaccurate. The validity of this concept was based on the British case, the fact that in the nineteenth century Britain, the workshop of the world, followed a policy of free trade, grew wealthy and, to a limited extent at least, made the rest of the world a wealthier place in the process. This model, a nation freely exchanging its manufactures for raw materials to the mutual benefit of all, was, however, on the Prebisch thesis an exceptional situation. It arose mainly because Britain was a country largely deficient in raw materials and therefore willing to accept imports freely, and uninterested in the possibility of developing substitutes for imports based on her own scanty natural resources.

In the twentieth century, however, the situation has been transformed. The typical workshop of the world is no longer Britain, but the United States, a country with large natural resources of her own, and a tradition of protectionism which encouraged exploitation of her own resources and the substitution, wherever possible, of home resources for imports. The rapid industrial expansion of such an economy thus carried few benefits for the raw-material producers. Apart from the fall in the relative quantity of imports, the situation was developed, for political and social reasons, where domestic agriculture was fostered at the expense of imports. As the standard of living of the industrial countries was raised the relative share spent on necessities requiring imports fell. As technological substitution grew and relative efficiency in using raw materials improved, the gap between the industrial nations and the raw-material exporter also grew. The rich grew richer, and the poorer nations were left farther and farther behind.

The free play of market forces which was envisaged in, among other schemes, the G.A.T.T. system is therefore relevant between nations which are structurally similar (i.e. between industrial country and industrial country), but is not applicable to the relationship between industrial nation and developing nation. This imbalance of power in negotiations between the developed and developing is not helped by the tendency to protectionism in the former; and the more recent tendencies to economic integration among the industrially advanced nations may worsen the imbalance.

Dr Prebisch argues that a target growth of at least five per cent per annum should be the aim for the developing nations by 1970. Five per cent might seem by British standards a fairly stiff target – it is more than the maximum which the N.E.D.C. seems to consider possible for Britain. But even at this rate, taking into consideration the rapid growth of population in many of these countries, it would take the best part of a century for many of these nations to reach even the present per capita standard of living of Western Europe. To reach the present standard of Western Europe by the end of the century would require a growth rate of seven to eight per cent.

Faced with these figures, even the optimist would quail. But this is by no means the end of the problem. To reach a four per cent growth rate in the United Kingdom requires at least a five per cent growth in exports. To reach the minimum five per cent growth of the developing nations' programme a six per cent growth in their exports would be required; and even this would suffice only so long as the prices paid for raw materials exported by them did not fall in relation to the price of manufactured goods which they had to buy. The conditions of the 1950s and early 1960s, however, suggest that this cannot be assumed with any confidence. About half the value of the increase in the developing countries' exports in this period was lost because raw-material prices did not keep pace with the prices of manufactured goods. This deterioration was undoubtedly due in no small degree to increased technological progress in the developed countries. Despite a change in 1962, a change which is in all probability temporary, the pace of technological advance of the developed countries – implying among other things less reliance on raw-material imports – is likely to increase rather than diminish. The growth in atomic power, automation and leisure, which appear to cause such problems of structural unemployment in the developed countries, is scarcely likely to bring much comfort to the developing nations.

To a large degree the development of the raw-material producers into manufacturing nations, their only hope of achieving any substantial rise in living standards, depends on their ability to acquire the foreign exchange which will permit them the essential imports of capital goods and services.

There are basically three methods whereby this might be achieved: through greater earnings from the export of raw materials; through increased exports of manufactured goods; or through greater loans or grants. Let us consider some of the implications of each of these.

About increased earnings from raw-material imports a good deal has been said elsewhere. But possibly the most damning point which can be made is that it is a reversal of the economic facts of life. To attempt to raise prices artificially, even with the consent of the importing nations, is merely to add further economic incentive to the technological process of substitution. Natural rubber is slowly losing ground to artificial rubber. Doubling the price of the former would merely speed the development of the latter. Oil is replacing coal and holding back the growth of atomic energy on economic grounds. To double the price of oil would expand the sales of one of the few raw materials available in Britain and would make atomic power a very much more attractive proposition. At the end of a decade of such policies would the exporters of rubber or oil find themselves any better off? The chances are rather that they would find that their exports had fallen not merely in volume, but even more in value.

Leaving aside for the moment the possible consequences of such a policy, how could higher prices be achieved? By one of two methods, presumably. The first would be by the use of commodity agreements designed to create a higher price for the commodity than already obtains. As has been remarked earlier, a problem of the commodity agreement with too high a price is that it will encourage over-production. To set the price too high, as a matter of deliberate policy, might well be to compound the error, and incidentally place the main burden of the aid programme on countries, like Britain, which are fairly liberal in their import policy towards raw materials, while leaving the country with a 'protectionist' policy on imports unscathed. And, equally important, the expansion would take place in the 'extractive' industries, rather than the industries which really need to be created to change developing nations into developed nations.

An alternative to the commodity agreement approach is the 'compensatory finance' approach, whereby some form of compensation, dispensed by an international organization, would be paid by developed countries to developing countries in respect of any deterioration in the earning ability of their exports caused by the technological developments which work so strongly in favour of the industrial nations. That such a system would have considerable advantages is undeniable – equally undeniable would be the immense political and economic problems attached to it.

A second suggestion, which was put forward in the Prebisch report, is that the flow of manufactured goods from developing to developed nations should be increased – a notion which appears to run counter to economic common sense. Yet when one considers the object of the exercise it makes a good deal of sense. To create industries one needs markets. So far as many of the developing nations are concerned, one finds a 'which comes first, the chicken or the egg' argument. A new industry needing a market will create one at home in time, in, say, a generation; but if it does not have an alternative market in the meantime, it simply will not survive. If, however, an industry can simultaneously protect its own nascent home market and have an entrée into an existing market – which can be found only in the developed nations – then it has the prospect of survival. The logic of encouraging industrialization in the developing nations must be to permit them free access to the markets of the developed nations – without incidentally any reciprocal freedom in the other direction being necessarily conceded.

The difficulty immediately arises, however, of deciding what type of manufactured goods are to be given free access to the markets of the developed nations. One has merely to look at the persistent demands for protection which have arisen in the cotton industry – for textile manufacturing is historically one of the first and easiest industries to create in a non-industrial society – to appreciate the difficulties. Cheap cotton goods are in practice subject to a good deal of import restriction in the developed countries, and any attempt to follow a more liberal policy will bring down the wrath of management and labour on any government with the temerity to do so.

And yet even textiles are a comparatively innocuous product. What would be the reaction to an attempt to encourage massive imports of commodities which have even more dangerous political or economic consequences? Would it be possible to encourage the British consumer to buy motor cars – and the idea of the motor car as an industry for an underdeveloped country is by no means ludicrous – or ships, television sets, electronic equipment of all sorts from the developing nations? Each one of these industries could be justified as being appropriate for the developing country; and each one would represent political dynamite.

Nevertheless there can be little doubt that a satisfactory solution to the problem of helping the developing countries by 'trade, not aid' will demand that the industrially advanced countries such as Britain accept increased imports of manufactured goods.

The final theme of the Prebisch plan is quite simply a plea for increased aid, be it by loans or grants. The type of aid which can be offered in this situation may be either unconditional, that is, without restrictions on where any grants and loans are spent, or 'tied', that is, aid which can only be taken in the form of goods and materials from the donor country.

How much aid should be given? The figure most widely quoted has been one per cent of a country's national income. The United Kingdom's share is only about two-thirds of this, France's twice as much, and there is no uniformity at all in the amounts pledged by the various countries.

On the paradoxical hostility that aid can create in the receiving country we have already commented. It is human to resent help –

even if it is not admirable. But there are ominous signs that, even as the need for aid is becoming more acute, resentment is being generated at the idea of giving aid to a vociferously ungrateful country. For every taxpayer in Britain, France or the United States who is enthusiastic about giving aid, there is probably at least one more who bitterly resents it.

The course of the Conference

The initial results of the U.N.T.A.D. Conference were a little disappointing. Some attempt had of course been made to turn the Conference into a theatre of the Cold War, but it became rather apparent that for East or West to attack the other could prove to be a two-edged weapon. One fact which emerged was the conflict of interest between the industrialized nations and the raw-material producers, and the Russians are in this situation as vulnerable to attack as the West. Indeed there is some prospect of a split here, as elsewhere, between the interests of China, an underdeveloped country *par excellence*, and the Soviet Union, the second most important industrial nation in the World.

So far as the industrial nations were concerned, there emerged fairly rapidly the signs of a profound difference of approach. The American authorities, who appeared to be unhappy about the whole concept of the Conference, in effect followed a very cautious line, promising very little in the way of concessions.

The French authorities came perhaps closer to the Prebisch approach, contemplating the possibility of higher prices for raw materials. This would in practice have been in line with France's existing commitments to her former colonies, for she was to some extent paying them prices above the world average for raw materials. The burden of the increased expenditure of this policy would presumably have fallen elsewhere.

The British point of view was perhaps a little more adventurous. Starting cautiously enough by defending the role of the General Agreement on Tariffs and Trade, and with a number of resolutions which, while liberal in principle, were a little vague in detail, Britain's proposal offered to extend the principle of Imperial Preference to all developing nations, provided that this was acceptable to its existing beneficiaries and so long as some arrangements were made to compensate the Commonwealth nations by the offer of concessions from other industrial nations similar to those they already enjoy in the British market. But like the other Western formulas it aroused little enthusiasm in the early stages.

From a shaky start, however, the Conference partially recovered; it was a Conference of some confusion, and some bitterness, but it was not a disastrous failure – a fate which might easily have overtaken it, and from which it was saved almost at the eleventh hour.

An interim assessment

In spite of the many unanswered questions, and the occasional echoes of the Cold War, the Conference was in the main successful, with both a promise and a threat for the future relationship between the rich nations and the poor.

The element of success lay in the fact that the Conference did not simply split asunder with bitter quarrels, either between the developed and underdeveloped, or among the underdeveloped nations themselves. The latter, some 77 of the 120 nations attending, finally achieved a measure of unity in their approach to the developed nations, and took the first steps towards the creation of a new United Nations economic agency, a trade secretariat in which the major voice would be that of the poorer nations.

The institution of the 'seventy-seven' club, the formulation of a common aim, if not entirely a common economic policy, was a triumph for the moderates, both within and outside the group. For the extremists (and there was a fair leavening of those among the underdeveloped) wished to use their voting power in an attempt to force the Conference to recommend the dissolution of G.A.T.T., the 'rich man's club', imposing in its place commitments for aid and preferential treatment. There was, of course, no real hope of these aims being realized even if the voting had gone as the extremists desired, for the commitments would have been quite unacceptable to the nations on whom they would have been imposed. But a majority vote on these lines, followed as it would have been by a point-blank refusal of the minority – the Western developed nations – to accept it, would have resulted in the break-up of the Conference and a disastrous split between the majority and the West. The proposals which were agreed at the eleventh hour were by no means entirely satisfactory to the West, but neither were they unacceptable.

The negotiations had confirmed the three-way split in the Western approach, among the French, the British and the Americans, with the latter the most inflexible of all in their hostility to preferential tariffs in any form, even to the poorer nations. The attitude was perhaps a throw-back of the American resentment, a generation before, of the prewar British Imperial Preference system; some system of preference for all the underdeveloped nations might have been introduced on Imperial Preference lines, had the British proposals proved acceptable, but the idea was shelved because of the American attitude.

The commitments, rather vague in detail, which the developed nations did accept include the desirability of about one per cent of the national product of such nations being made available to aid the developing nations: this had been accepted in principle in the past, even if the aim had not always been achieved. In addition there were to be discussions on methods of achieving compensation for countries whose export earnings were adversely affected by technological change: a proposal to inhibit the development of synthetic substitutes for raw materials fortunately got nowhere.

As remarkable as anything at the Conference was the almost complete inability of the Soviet Bloc to harness the hostility of poorer nations towards the West. The 'poor-nation' majority seemed at times indifferent to the ideological distinctions between the developed nations. The Russians, in short, were tarred with the same brush as the capitalistic West, comparative affluence. Indeed so far were the Russians from achieving any substantial gains at the expense of the West that they found member nations of the Soviet Bloc showing increasing independence from Moscow, and even flirting with the possibility of joining G.A.T.T. rather than destroying it.

That the Conference did not wreck itself was, from the point of view of the West, a significant gain. That the moderates in the underdeveloped nations remained in control meant that, even if for the first time the poorer nations were collaborating effectively with each other, there was a possibility of cooperation, rather than downright hostility, between rich and poor.

But there were unfortunate undertones to the Conference. If the East–West Cold War had been successfully excluded, there was the possibility of a new split, between North and South, between the rich nations and the poor. The fact that the moderates had been able to achieve ascendancy at the Conference was no guarantee that they would continue to represent the underdeveloped nations; if the new U.N. agency achieved little concrete success there was the ominous possibility of a North–South racial split. Perhaps the fissures which were appearing in both the Western and Communist blocs would prove to be temporary, and the new-found unity of the underprivileged nations equally temporary. But the unity of the latter might become a unity against the West, and possibly against the European Communist bloc too. The political centre of gravity of the world might conceivably be changing, with incalculable results for the richer nations.

A second conference in New Delhi in 1968 in fact saw little new progress. The developed countries, both Western and Communist, were perhaps too preoccupied by their own internal and foreign problems to pay much attention to the problems of the underdeveloped nations.

But in spite of the lack of spectacular development during the middle 1960s, there is little doubt that the potential rift posed a problem which was likely to overshadow the remainder of the century.

If this North–South split on racial grounds is to be avoided, any contribution which Britain can make through her Commonwealth links may involve her in one of the most important roles which history has yet thrust upon her.

FURTHER READING – SOME SUGGESTIONS

Books and articles on the subjects discussed in this book abound. Those mentioned below scarcely make up an exhaustive or even entirely representative survey, but in general they have the merit of being readable without requiring too great a knowledge of economics from the non-specialist. The books are discussed in the context of the most appropriate chapter but the subject-matter is no more strictly confined to the single chapter than are the topics discussed in the book.

The first chapter deals in general terms with the world economy. For a historical approach to the development of the world economy two books might furnish a general introduction, W. Ashworth, *The International Economy since 1850* (Longmans, 1962), and W. A. Lewis, *Economic Survey 1919–39* (Allen & Unwin, 1949). The postwar developments are more generally covered in the appropriate chapters, but a useful start might be made with W. M. Scammel, *International Monetary Policy* (Macmillan, 1961).

The role of sterling in the world economy can to some extent also be approached from the historical angle. Sir Albert Feaver-year, *The Pound Sterling*, revised by E. V. Morgan (Oxford, 1963), is particularly appropriate in the latter part of the book dealing with sterling in the twentieth century.

The Sterling Area system is a concept which has changed its meaning almost decade by decade. Books which discuss the Sterling Area in the early postwar years, when it was perhaps of most significance, are R. N. Gardner, *Sterling–Dollar Diplomacy* (Oxford, 1956), dealing with the negotiations setting up the post-war monetary system in the 1940s; A. R. Conan, *The Sterling Area* (Macmillan, 1952), and P. W. Bell, *The Sterling Area in the Postwar World* (Oxford, 1956). Gardner and Bell are Americans and their assessment of the merits or demerits of the system have the advantage of being perhaps more detached from the situation than some British books.

The situation in the 1950s before the return to general convertibility is probably of less interest than the decades preceding and succeeding. For the interested reader, however, an excellent starting point would be A. C. L. Day, *The Future of Sterling* (Oxford, 1954), inevitably dated now since the situation has changed, but with a prescient view of the problems which have arisen since. Sir Roy Harrod has produced a series of articles providing a commentary on the various sterling crises, and these have been gathered into book form in *Topical Comment* and *Policy Against Inflation* (Macmillan). Finally for assessments of the Sterling Area in the late 1950s and 1960s there are A. R. Conan, *Rationale of the Sterling Area* (Macmillan, 1961) and C. McMahon, *Sterling in the Sixties* (Oxford, 1964).

To separate a discussion of the Sterling Area from the question of Britain's balance of payments is particularly artificial. The books suggested for the latter subject therefore inevitably cover a wider area than the subject of balance of payments. Two Penguins could provide an introduction, P. Einzig, *Monetary Policy: Ends and Means*, and A. Shonfield, *British Economic Policy Since the War*. More specific to the theme of balance of payments are N. Crump, *A.B.C. of the Foreign Exchanges* (Macmillan, 1963), and P. B. Kenen, *British Monetary Policy and the Balance of Payments* (Harvard, 1960), though the latter is more appropriate to the specialist reader.

There is a vast and constantly growing library on the subject of Britain and Europe. For a historical introduction the new reader might well begin with R. Mayne, *The Community of Europe* (Gollancz, 1962). A detailed account of British negotiations with the Six is to be found in M. Camps, *Britain and the European Community 1956–63* (1964), as authoritative an account as anything available. A shorter work is J. Pinder, *Britain and the Common Market* (Cresset, 1961). For an assessment of the probable effects of the movement towards European integration, U. Kitzinger, *The Challenge of the Common Market* (Blackwell,

1961), and the Economist Intelligence Unit's *The Commonwealth and Europe* and *If Britain Joins* provide a useful starting point. For various viewpoints of the situation there are E. Benoit, *Europe at Sixes and Sevens* (Columbia, 1961), R. E. Deniau, *The Common Market*, and F. V. Meyer, *The Seven* (Barrie & Rockliff with Pall Mall, 1962 and 1960). This subject is so dynamic, however, that almost every book published is overtaken by events.

In the subject of international equilibrium, particularly in respect of international liquidity, a useful start can be made with B. Tew, *International Monetary Co-operation 1945–63* (Hutchinson, 1963), and more recently Sir Roy Harrod, *Reforming the World's Money* (Macmillan, 1965). Other studies of the proposals to reform the International Monetary Fund may be found in R. Triffin, *Europe and the Money Muddle* and *Gold and the Dollar Crisis* (Yale). The study of the various proposals to amend the Fund is rapidly becoming a full-time occupation for the interested economists, and extracts from the leading advocates of change can be found in H. G. Grubel, *World Monetary Reform* (Oxford, 1963).

On trade and tariffs there are few if any satisfactory but nonspecialist books. Many economic textbooks deal with the subject in general terms, but detailed discussions on either the impact of tariffs, or the problems of customs unions generally presuppose a certain amount of prior knowledge of economics together with tenacity in reading.

The literature on the developing nations is also rapidly expanding. A useful introduction will be found in *The Economics of Underdeveloped Countries* by P. T. Bauer and B. S. Yamey (Cambridge, 1957). Bauer has more recently produced *Economic Analysis and Policy in Underdeveloped Countries* (Routledge & Kegan Paul, 1965), though this is perhaps more specialist in approach. Colin Clark, *Conditions of Economic Progress* (Macmillan, 1957), and A. K. Cairncross, *Factors in Economic Development* (Allen & Unwin, 1962), are more general, but they highlight the problems facing developing countries. On the subject of growth in general, W. Rostow, *Process of Economic Growth* (Oxford, 1960), and *The Stages of Economic Growth* (Cambridge, 1960), gives an American approach to the problem. More directly applicable to the developing nations are A. Shonfield, *The Attack on World Poverty* (Chatto, 1960), and the U.N. publication *Towards a New Trade Policy for Development* (1964).

Finally, anyone who is interested enough to read this book will probably be aware of just how much is written week by week in the financial sections of the 'quality Sundays', the *Sunday Times*, *Sunday Telegraph* and the *Observer*. And if any reader interested in the subject is not a regular reader of the *Economist* he would be well advised to begin now.

INDEX

INDEX

MORE ABOUT PENGUINS
AND PELICANS

Penguinews, which appears every month, contains details of all the new books issued by Penguins as they are published. From time to time it is supplemented by *Penguins in Print* – a complete list of all our available titles. (There are well over three thousand of these.)

A specimen copy of *Penguinews* will be sent to you free on request, and you can become a subscriber for the price of the postage – 4s. for a year's issues (including the complete lists) if you live in the United Kingdom, or 8s. if you live elsewhere. Just write to Dept EP, Penguin Books Ltd, Harmondsworth, Middlesex, enclosing a cheque or postal order, and your name will be added to the mailing list.

Some other books published by Penguins are described on the following pages.

Note: *Penguinews* and *Penguins in Print* are not available in the U.S.A. or Canada

ECONOMIC PLANNING AND DEMOCRACY

Firmin Oulès

The currents of economic planning and democratic freedom run counter. Hence one of our acutest dilemmas.

Professor Oulès, leader of 'The New Lausanne School' of economists, faces this difficulty squarely in a new Pelican in which he effectively 'demystifies' the economic complex of Western Europe, laying bare the forces which determine the array of facts and figures we call economics. His examination is both honest and intelligent, and he comments forcefully on the anti-democratic trend of 'indicative planning', as practised notably in France.

As an alternative Professor Oulès makes his own recommendation. It is for 'planning by enlightenment' – a concept which combines budgetary co-ordination, at the national level, with the systematic provision of enough data for industry, finance, commerce, and labour to act rationally yet freely.

Economic Planning and Democracy is at once a brilliantly clear exposition of the material realities of trade and industry and a constructive solution of a problem which is today admitted by most politicians and economists.

INDUSTRY IN THE U.S.A.

Geoffrey Owen

What is it that places American industry, as a whole, so far ahead of the world? The talent of businessmen, the good sense of unions, the attitude of government, or just a wealth of raw materials? This new Pelican takes a dispassionate look at industrial research and organization in America, at the level of capital investment, and at training for management (as offered, say, by the Harvard Business School): are these, asks the author, notably superior to what we find in Europe?

In particular the book isolates one factor which could account for much of America's lead – the respect (if not veneration) in which industry and commerce are held throughout the United States.

Geoffrey Owen represented the *Financial Times* in America for three years before his appointment as Industrial Editor. In this study of the roots of the American success story, he compares the men and methods he saw at work there with their European counterparts.

THE ECONOMICS OF EVERYDAY
LIFE

Gertrude Williams

'It is a measure of her success that she makes the whole subject sound like very little more than applied commonsense,
but commonsense applied to familiar situations in a way that
picks out a consistent pattern and shows the reader that the
"economic aspect" is nothing more abstruse than a methodi-
cal selection from facts which, in a muddle-headed way, he
knows already' – *Economist*

The title of this book reveals its intention – to analyse in
plain, non-technical language some of the important economic issues which affect life today in Britain. Now revised and
brought completely up-to-date to include the National Incomes Commission of 1962, the unemployment crisis of 1963,
and other important economic developments, this book deals
with matters that are of interest to everybody because they
are closely allied to the daily life of the individual. Why do
prices go up and down? Who really pays for advertisements?
Is monopoly anti-social? These and many other vital questions are discussed in such a way that the reader is able to
understand the complex factors involved in trying to reach
sensible answers.

THE ECONOMIC HISTORY OF
WORLD POPULATION
Carlo M. Cipolla

This book presents a global view of the demographic and economic development of mankind.

Professor Cipolla has deliberately adopted a new point of view and has tried to trace the history of the great trends in population and wealth which have affected mankind as a whole. For it would have been inadequate to regard such a global history as being merely the sum total of national economic histories in abridged form.

Among the massive problems that face the human race the author emphasizes the demographic explosion, the economic backwardness of vast areas, the spread of industrial revolution and of technical knowledge. Whilst the theoretical approach can help our analysis of these problems, Professor Cipolla believes that they can only be wholly grasped and solved when they are studied in their full historical perspective.